SOMEONE TO TURN TO

SOMEONE
TO
TURN TO

Experiences
of Help
before Divorce

Ann K Mitchell

ABERDEEN UNIVERSITY PRESS

First published 1981
Aberdeen University Press
A member of the Pergamon Group
© Ann K Mitchell 1981

British Library Cataloguing in Publication Data
Mitchell, Ann K
  Someone to turn to.
  1. Divorce—Great Britain
  2. Married people—Services for—Great Britain
  I. Title
  362.8'2 HQ875
  ISBN 0 08 025741 0

PRINTED IN GREAT BRITAIN AT
ABERDEEN UNIVERSITY PRESS

CONTENTS

TABLES

ACKNOWLEDGEMENTS

This research was made possible by the willing co-operation of the divorced men and women who kindly agreed to be interviewed, and who deserve my special thanks.

I am greatly indebted to Professor John Spencer, of the Department of Social Administration in the University of Edinburgh, who died in June 1978, for suggesting that I should look at the pre-divorce experiences of both partners in, perhaps, a hundred Scottish divorces. Such a study could usefully follow my 18 years as a voluntary worker in marriage guidance, as counsellor and administrator. At an early stage, the permission of the Court of Session was sought, and the project was approved.

Valuable support was given to me by Professor Spencer, by Dr Michael Anderson (Department of Sociology, and now Professor of Economic History) and, latterly, by Ralph Davidson all of whom supervised the work of my subsequent postgraduate research degree. I am grateful, too, for discussions with Dr (now Professor) Eric Clive (Department of Scots Law) and Professor Christopher Turner (Department of Sociology, University of Stirling).

The Central Council for Education and Training in Social Work generously awarded me a research fellowship for the first year of the research. Gaps in my knowledge of divorce procedure were patiently filled by a number of legal practitioners, especially Norma Morgan, Sheriff-Principal Robert Reid, Q.C. and Jonathan Mitchell.

Some of the material in this book has been published in articles in *Marriage Guidance,* in the *Journal of the Law Society of Scotland* and in *The Sociological Review.*

I am grateful to Nancy Drucker for advice on the final draft of the book, and to Valerie Chuter for her impeccable typing.

Finally, I want to thank Angus, my husband, without whose unfailing interest and encouragement the work could not have been accomplished.

NOTE ON TERMINOLOGY

In Scotland, the two parties to a divorce are the pursuer and the defender (equivalent to the petitioner and the respondent in England and Wales). A husband-pursuer is therefore a husband who is the pursuer in a divorce action.

Throughout the book, the divorced people who were interviewed are described as the respondents.

For convenience in analysis, mentions of parents with custody of their children refer to *de facto* custody, i.e. to the parents with whom children were living at the time of divorce. The court is not required to make an order for custody, and some parents make no application.

CHAPTER 1

INTRODUCTION

THE AIM OF THE RESEARCH

This is an attempt to discover from whom recently divorced couples had sought or received help when their marriages broke down. On the evidence from a small sample, some policy recommendations can be made and some areas requiring further research can be indicated.

'Help' can have many different meanings. In the context of marital breakdown, it has here been taken to cover practical help, emotional support and professional advice. It was left to respondents in the subsequent survey to interpret the word 'help' as they liked. I judged it expedient to try not to impose my own ideas of what constituted help but to use this deliberately loose description and to allow respondents to make their own definitions. What seemed to me to be important might not have been similarly viewed by the respondents. Some relevant topics may not have been sufficiently explored, but it seemed that the quality of the interview material would be better if rigid definitions of 'help' were not used. Similarly, I did not explicitly define problems for which help might have been needed, but allowed respondents freedom to recall what seemed relevant to them.

There is formal provision of legal, medical and social work services for those whose marriages break down, in addition to services available from voluntary organisations. The providers of such services will know of the existing demand for them but may know neither the opinions of their clients nor the extent of any unmet need.

The Finer Committee on One-Parent Families (1974, para 8.55), found a bewildering array of services which might be used by one-parent families. The Committee recommended that information about such services should be more readily available. Morris, Cooper and Byles (1973) investigated how people decide when, and from whom, to seek help with legal problems. Their strongest impressions were of a lack of knowledge of legal and social services available, the resignation with which people accepted their situation, and the overlap between social and legal problems. Lawyers, who were believed to charge fees, were seen as likely to be less dedicated than doctors.

A conclusion reached by Brandwein, Brown and Fox (1974) that 'formal institutions appear unwilling and unable to provide emotional supports' was different from Blaxter's. She was concerned with problems relating to disability and wrote: 'The

1

majority of doctors ... recognised how often social problems lay behind the
medical problems presented to them, and they were willing and anxious to offer
personal support ... (but) did not see themselves as part of a larger network of
services' (Blaxter, 1976). She also found an ambivalence between social workers
and clients: 'Whereas the social workers saw themselves as helping agents, the
potential clients saw them as arbitrating and inspecting officials almost exclusively concerned with financial aid'. Misperceptions of professional aid are no
doubt widespread.

There is also an informal network of family, friends and neighbours which might be
called upon to support broken marriages and to complement any professional support.

Mayer and Timms (1970) considered that both informal and professional sources of
support should be examined simultaneously: they could be seen as alternatives, and
respondents who were sufficiently supported by an informal network might have less
need for professional services.

The Wolfenden Committee on the future of voluntary organisations (1978) reported a
paucity of knowledge about such informal social services, but considered the
extent to be considerable. The Committee suggested that statutory and voluntary
organisations should 'develop policies which more consistently and deliberately
support the informal system'.

Family studies (e.g. Bott, 1957; Klein, 1965; Young and Wilmott, 1957) have described the value of such informal networks. Studies of behaviour in specific
crises also emphasise the importance of the family.

Townsend (1957) found in his East London sample that a higher proportion of the
elderly in hospital or in residential homes than in the community had no surviving
children, and especially no surviving daughters. He was led to the conclusion that,
among the elderly, the heaviest claims on health and social services were made by
those with no female relatives living nearby. In a later, national, survey
Townsend and Wedderburn (1965) reported that 'in illness and infirmity the role of
the family in providing personal and household care dwarfs that of the social
services', but that a great many old people who appeared to qualify for, and feel
a need for, social services were not receiving them.

Morris's prisoners' wives (Morris, 1965) who had reported contacts with social
work agencies (mostly probation officers or prison welfare staff) mainly described
initial advice or assistance but nothing further, which left them feeling unsupported. These wives also reported some hostility from their parents and from
near neighbours. This had led to ambivalent relationships with some parents, who
had offered housing or financial help but not sympathy. More wives had been
supported by friends or siblings than by parents.

Parkes (1972) suggested that friends or neighbours may be more useful than
families in bereavement: 'It may be easier to talk to outsiders about problems
which threaten self-esteem' but 'clergy, like everyone else, are often embarrassed
and ineffectual'.

Moyes (1976) found that women experiencing their first pregnancies had not liked
to ask many questions of their doctors, from fear of being ridiculed for apparent
ignorance. Instead, they had usually turned for information to other women who had
had babies, but particularly to their contemporaries - their sisters, friends or
work-mates. It was sometimes seen as inappropriate to discuss sexual matters with
their mothers.

It is clearly important that help of various kinds should be available at a time of marital breakdown for those who need it during their transition from the married to the divorced state. At the same time as the demand for such services might be expected to be increasing because of the greater incidence of divorce, some services might well be decreasing because of financial stringencies. Planning legal, social work and other services for future divorcing couples could take into account the experience of those recently divorced.

This study looks only at those whose marriages ended in divorce. It does not look at those whose marriages survived stressful periods, at those who separated but for some reason did not proceed to divorce, nor at those in the grey area in between, who continued to live out their dead marriages because they could not see a viable alternative. All of them might have needed the same range of help or support which is here investigated.

PREVIOUS RESEARCH

Previous research based on interviews with spouses from broken marriages has tended to be concerned with either husbands or wives and more often only with wives. Chester (1975), Goode (1956) and Marsden (1969) all interviewed wives only and George and Wilding (1972) fathers only (including widowers). Ferri and Robinson (1976) interviewed widowed as well as divorced or separated single parents, including both fathers and mothers. Elston, Fuller and Murch (1975) and Hart (1976) interviewed divorced men and women, but the former were all petitioners and Hart's sample was self-selected.

An important study of a divorced population was by Goode (1956) who, in 1948, carried out a survey in Detroit of the post-divorce adjustment of 425 mothers aged 20 to 30 at the time of divorce.

He investigated the pre-marriage, marriage and post-marriage lives of his respondents, and paid detailed attention to their finances. Many of his questions were problem-orientated, investigating the effect of marital breakdown on health, access to social activities, and care of children, and appeared to throw little light on relationships with potential helpers. He paid more attention to the characteristics of those who divorce than to their personal attitudes and needs.

Goode found, as others have done, that trauma tended to be associated with separation rather than with other stages of the divorce process. A formidable interviewing schedule was used, with 120 questions, including some multi-choice and some open-ended, and interviews lasted upwards of one and a half hours. He used four time-cohorts, of those divorced for 2, 8, 14 and 26 months. He later thought it would have been more illuminating to have used only one of these cohorts and to have interviewed the same people three times, but realised that a considerable number might have changed addresses and become lost.

There have been few research projects in Britain based on interviews with a divorced population.

Chester (1975), who examined the court records of all divorces in Hull over a three year period, 1966-68, later had intensive interviews with 210 women petitioners (i.e. pursuers). He had permission from the Lord Chancellor's office to have direct access to court files in Hull, provided that he did not record names and addresses. From transcriptions of 1500 divorces in 1966-68 he studied 1000 to investigate the characteristics of those who divorce. He also advertised in the Guardian, Observer, New Society and New Statesman, resulting in 200 divorcees writing for him extended accounts of their personal experiences, and answering a brief questionnaire.

Although Chester did not have access to names and addresses in the court files, he was able to obtain these from the Hull Daily Mail which prints lists of divorces granted. For his sample to be interviewed, he took three time-cohorts, divorced for 9 months, 21 months and 33 months. His aim was to collect and analyse age at marriage, duration of marriage, education, occupation, birth rank and size of family of origin, stability of parental marriage, length of acquaintance and courtship, preparation for marriage, type of ceremony, fertility and premarital pregnancy. He also examined pre-divorce discussion and the use of conciliation agencies, and his interviews with women petitioners lasted from $2\frac{1}{2}$ to $3\frac{1}{2}$ hours, often apparently being a cathartic experience for the women. He later regretted relating his time cohorts to the date of divorce, which was of less relevance than the date of separation. The interval between separation and divorce was more stressful than the divorce action itself, a finding which supported Goode's earlier experience. Chester's sample showed a lack of pre-divorce discussion between spouses. Only 11 per cent had discussed any details with their husbands. Rather more (15 per cent) had consulted marriage guidance counsellors before separation and 8 per cent had consulted probation officers.

Elston, Fuller and Murch (1975) investigated the circumstances of families in divorce proceedings. The Lord Chancellor refused them access to court records, but allowed them to sit in court and take down petitioners' names and addresses. They took a random sample in three courts of one in three of undefended divorces with dependent children, during January to June 1973. They wrote to 145 petitioners, requesting an interview to ask about 'experience of the procedure of getting divorced, ... to study the way the new divorce laws are working'. Interviews were obtained with 102 petitioners in their own homes for an average of $2\frac{1}{2}$ hours. Most of the interviews were tape-recorded. The sample were asked (Murch, 1975) whether they had consulted anyone about their marriage difficulties, separating professional or semi-professional help from that given by relatives and friends. They were asked which had been most helpful in each of these two categories, but not about the kind of help sought or given.

Murch found that family doctors were of key importance to those getting divorced, and he recommended that they should be enabled to have better understanding of marital tensions. He suggested that the legal profession is too little concerned with the future of children in divorce, in spite of claiming that their interests are paramount. He considered that marriage guidance counsellors would never be able to change the public's image of them as marriage-savers, and that they should concentrate their services on those who need help within marriage. Finally, he saw a need for a pre-divorce counselling service, preferably affiliated in some way to the courts, and using a combination of the skills of a marriage guidance counsellor with those of the existing Divorce Court welfare officer (a post which has never existed in Scotland). However, not only was this written for English courts, but it was before the new procedure whereby most English divorces are dealt with by post. Murch published his findings on the role of solicitors in divorce proceedings (Murch, 1977) in which he compared the opinions of legal services of his original sample of 102 petitioners with those of 41 couples whose names were given to him by Divorce Court welfare officers because their children had been the subject of welfare reports. He concluded that most of the clients in both samples had been satisfied with the services of their solicitors, who had often also provided a modicum of emotional support in a time of crisis.

During 1968-69, Hart recorded interviews with 62 men and women members of a club for the divorced and separated, and also made observations of meetings of the club (Hart, 1976). Her main concern was to study the process of adjustment from the status of being married to that of being separated or divorced, within a self-selected group, admitted to be atypical. The members of the club remained conscious of belonging to 'a minority association of social deviants'. She examined the

institution of marriage, common expectations and the reasons for conflict, but did
not discuss the club members' experiences of helping agencies. However, she did
ask her respondents to whom they had first turned for help, and the replies
included 46 per cent 'family', 14 per cent 'friend', 9 per cent 'other' and 22 per
cent 'no one'. No professions or agencies were specified.

One other research study concluded with a small number of interviews with separated
men and women. Professor McGregor and his colleagues undertook a survey of
magistrates' matrimonial jurisdiction, with a preliminary exploration of its social
results (McGregor, Blom-Cooper and Gibson, 1970). Since court records could throw
no light on feelings and attitudes of spouses, the authors arranged for a jour-
nalist to publish an article in the News of the World in 1967, appealing for
information from 'victims of broken homes'. They sent a questionnaire to the 523
husbands and 484 wives who replied to the article and who had had experience of
magistrates' matrimonial jurisdiction but who were not yet divorced. The postal
response from this self-selected sample was 60 per cent for husbands and 71 per
cent for wives. From 544 returned questionnaires 48 per cent had consulted a
solicitor, 34 per cent a Probation Officer, 25 per cent a doctor, 16 per cent a
clergyman and 11 per cent a marriage guidance counsellor.

The only published research relating to divorces in Scotland is in Eekelaar and
Clive (1977). Dr (now Professor) Clive examined a one in thirty sample of all
those divorces granted in Scotland in 1975 where there were children under 16. His
purpose was to find out, by studying court records, how the court had dealt with
the custody of the children in these 203 divorces.

Eekelaar and Clive reported, of Scottish divorces, 'it appears that judges are
prepared to indicate their satisfaction with the arrangements for the children on
the scantiest of information' (para 13.4). The court usually accepted the word of
the pursuer that the children were happy and well cared-for, even when they were
resident with the defender who was not present in, nor represented in, court
(para 8.1). The research showed that custody was awarded to the wife in 78.8 per
cent of these Scottish divorces and to the husband in 8.9 per cent. In over 10 per
cent of cases, no custody order had been made. It was rare for a pursuer to suggest
a change in the status quo; and if a pursuer did not have the children living with
him, he seldom made any proposals for custody. In Scotland, it was not usually
possible to tell from the court records whether access was being exercised at the
time of the summons, since no information had been sought on the subject. In only
8 per cent of the Scottish cases was there any legal provision for access after
divorce. In only six cases (3 per cent), in all of which there had been a
parental dispute about custody, did the court ask for a report on the welfare of
the children. These reports were all written by advocates. Far more information
about children was available in the English divorces studied, where there was also
greater willingness to investigate custody arrangements, with reports by welfare
officers in 11.3 per cent, most of them having no dispute about custody or access.
Nevertheless, the authors found no difference in outcome between England and
Scotland because 'it was so rare for courts in either jurisdiction to make an
order which altered the child's residence' (para 13.23).

Some services for single parent families in Edinburgh have been highlighted by
Hopkinson (1976) and Humphries (1976). The first of these studies examined the
experiences of single mothers with illegitimate babies, and the second described
an experimental project which brought together single parent families and volunteers.

Hopkinson interviewed 116 single mothers in hospital and again (whenever possible)
three, six and twelve months after the birth of their babies. She investigated the
background of the mothers and of the fathers, and the reactions of the mothers'

families to the new babies. She described housing, financial and employment
problems, and looked at facilities for day care of the babies and for a social
life for the mothers. While she found the mothers' families to be generally
supportive, social workers mostly gave practical assistance in a crisis but not
continuing support.

The project described by Humphries was the development of the use of volunteers to
befriend single parents and to help them to plan their future and to make use of
available services. She reported that the volunteers helped the families to an
appreciable extent in the ways in which they perceived their situation and in
increasing their social contacts. Volunteers were seen by the families to be
friends, whereas social workers from the same agency were viewed as authority
figures.

When the fieldwork and most of the analysis for the present study had been
completed, another study was published about the characteristics of those who get
divorced (Thornes and Collard, 1979). In a comparison of interviews with a
divorced population and with a still married one, combinations of factors were
found to predispose towards divorce. Teenage marriage and premarital pregnancy
were, predictably, found to be high-risk factors, and particularly if combined
with parental opposition to the marriage. Other findings were that marriages in
which wives were only children or in which husbands had no sister may be slightly
prone to divorce. Parental divorce did not appear to lead to divorce in the next
generation unless the children had been under five at the time of their parents'
divorce. The authors found that problems leading to marriage breakdown tended to
start early in the marriage (in the first year for one third of their divorced
sample and in the first five years for three quarters of the sample). They
emphasised that their findings were not conclusive, but could only point to some
kinds of marriage which might be divorce-prone.

Although increasing numbers of marriages are ending in divorce, there is a paucity
of research about the experiences of support received by men and women prior to
divorce. A Home Office consultative document by the Working Party on Marriage
Guidance (1979) stated that 'little accurate information exists about ... how many
people turn for help, where they seek it, and with what result' (para 3.3).

                    LAW OF DIVORCE IN SCOTLAND

Scottish divorce jurisdiction has been based exclusively in Edinburgh since 1563
(in the Commissary Court until 1830 and thereafter in the Court of Session) (Clive
and Wilson, 1974). Since the Reformation, divorce has been equally available to
husbands and to wives, on grounds of adultery or desertion. In England a wife has
had the same access to divorce as her husband only since 1923, having previously
had to prove desertion or cruelty in addition to adultery. Divorce for desertion
was not available in England until 1938.

A Royal Commission on the law of divorce in England was appointed in 1850, and the
Lord Advocate gave evidence about the law in Scotland (Royal Commission on Law of
Divorce, 1853). A paper on divorce in Scotland was also presented to the Royal
Commission, stating that the Court of Session had 'pronounced 95 sentences of
divorce' from November 1836 to November 1841. The names of both parties to these
95 divorces, including the maiden name of wives and occupations and home towns of
husbands, were recorded and preserved for posterity by the Royal Commission, which
took these details from the Law Magazine, May 1843. They were 'almost all of the
humbler classes ... except in a single instance not one of the Scottish gentry'.
In over one third, 'the sentence of divorce was at the suit of the wife against
the husband'. Occupations included carver, hatter, saddler, teacher of music,

butler, quill seller and journeyman tinsmith.

Scottish judicial statistics were published for the first time in 1869, but gave
no classification of divorces until 1898, in which year there were 153 divorce
actions, of which 19 were defended (Royal Commission on Marriage and Divorce, 1912,
para 6192). Of decrees granted in that year, 77 were on grounds of desertion
(raised mainly by the wife) and 68 on grounds of adultery (raised mainly by the
husband).

In 1912, the higher divorce rate in Scotland compared with that in England had
four explanations: the existence since 1424 of the 'poor's roll', cheaper proceedings (£25 to £30 for an undefended action, excluding witness's expenses), the
existence of desertion as a ground for divorce, and equality between the spouses
in the availability of divorce (Royal Commission on Marriage and Divorce, 1912,
paras 6223 ff). In 1906/7, one third of divorce actions in Scotland were thought
to have been raised with legal assistance from the poor's roll (para 6273). The
poor's roll made divorce available to those of limited financial means by providing free services of solicitors and advocates. Unlike the present Legal Aid
system, a wife had to rely on her husband's credit if he had sufficient financial
means, and therefore the earlier system benefited most those divorces where both
spouses were eligible for admission to the poor's roll (Clive and Wilson, 1974).

In spite of the Royal Commission's majority recommendation to extend the principle
of the matrimonial offence, there was no change in the law of divorce in Scotland
until 1938, when cruelty, sodomy, bestiality and incurable insanity became
additional grounds for divorce (Divorce (Scotland) Act 1938). Desertion then
gradually declined as a ground to only 14 per cent of Scottish divorces granted in
1976 (Civil Judicial Statistics, Scotland, 1976). Increased acceptance by judges
of evidence of cruelty led to this becoming the most common ground for divorce,
from 5 per cent of all actions in 1950 to 49 per cent in 1976 (Scottish Law
Commission, 1967). The Morton Commission, in 1956, recommended the retention of
the concept of a matrimonial offence for divorce in Scotland, with the addition of
'conduct of a grave and weighty nature on the part of one spouse which is such
that the other spouse could not in the face of it reasonably be expected to
continue with the conjugal life ... where it has resulted in the separation of the
spouses (other than by agreement) for a period of three years or more' (Royal
Commission on Marriage and Divorce, 1956, para 170). The members of the Commission
were equally divided on whether divorce should be allowed for irretrievable breakdown where no matrimonial offence had been committed. Again, no legislation
followed.

In 1967 the Scottish Law Commission recommended the retention of the existing
grounds for divorce, while substituting for 'cruelty' 'conduct of a character so
intolerable as to make it unreasonable to expect the pursuer to adhere' and
reducing the period of desertion from three years to two (Scottish Law Commission,
1967). The members further recommended granting divorce on the grounds of
irretrievable breakdown of marriage, after two years of separation if both parties
consented or for some longer period if one party did not consent.

The General Assembly of the Church of Scotland accepted a recommendation by the
Social and Moral Welfare Board in 1969 that breakdown of marriage should be the
sole ground for divorce, evidence of breakdown being separation for two years
(Church of Scotland, 1969).

There followed seven unsuccessful Private Members' Bills to change the law of
divorce in Scotland, the legal concept of a matrimonial offence as ground for
divorce continuing until 1 January 1977, six years later than reform in England
and Wales.

The Divorce (Scotland) Act 1976 provided for divorce only where a marriage had
broken down irretrievably. Breakdown was to be established by evidence of adultery,
unreasonable behaviour, two years' desertion, two years' separation where the
defender consents to divorce or five years' separation without the defender's
consent to divorce.

Fears appear to have been groundless that divorce by consent or unilateral divorce
without the defender's consent would lead to an immediate sharp rise in the number
of divorces granted, as had happened in England. There, a previous slow though
accelerating annual increase in divorces granted changed to a more than 100 per
cent increase in 1971, with a further 50 per cent increase by 1977.

Scottish divorces granted in 1977 were nearly equally divided between pre-1976
legislation and the 1976 Act (Civil Judicial Statistics, Scotland, 1977). The total
number was 8812, an increase of only 1.7 per cent over the previous year. Although
divorces were, for the first time, granted throughout the summer vacation in 1978,
the number of decrees granted during the second half of 1978 was substantially less
than during the similar period in 1977 (Swinton and Clark, 1977).

There are no decrees nisi and absolute in Scotland, but there is a three week delay
in issuing a divorce certificate to allow time for an appeal on new evidence (Clive
and Wilson, 1974). The parties to a divorce are wiser not to remarry until the
expiry of the three week period.

                    THE DIVORCE PROCEDURE

Anyone wanting to obtain a divorce in Scotland must use a solicitor; anyone living
outside Edinburgh must have a local solicitor who, in turn, must use an Edinburgh
one as his agent in dealing with the court. The Edinburgh solicitor normally
engages an advocate to draft the summons.

At the first interview with a solicitor, the client is asked for full names of
both parties, their ages, address(es), occupations, incomes, names and ages of
children of the marriage, date of marriage and date of separation (if any) (Keith
and Clark, 1977). If the last date is recent, a divorce on grounds of separation
or desertion is not possible, and the client is asked whether the spouse has been
associating with someone else. If not, the only remaining cause of breakdown of
the marriage is unreasonable behaviour, and the client is asked to give details.
This can be painful, but the solicitor explains that it is necessary in order to
produce evidence for divorce.

The solicitor applies for a Legal Aid certificate if necessary (and this can cause
a two or three months delay). Next he normally asks an advocate to draft a summons
and sends one copy to the pursuer, or asks the pursuer to come and discuss it, to
make sure that it is understood and that the details are correct. The solicitor
sends a copy of the summons to the Court of Session for signetting, and fourteen
days later another copy is served on the defender, usually by recorded delivery.

The preamble to a summons is:

> Elizabeth II, by the Grace of God, of the United Kingdom of
> Great Britain and Northern Ireland and of Her other Realms
> and Territories Queen, Head of the Commonwealth, Defender
> of the Faith, to the said ... : Whereas by this Summons the
> pursuer craves the Lords of our Council and Session to
> pronounce against you in terms of the conclusion appended
> hereto, We therefore charge you that, if you have any good

reasons why such decree should not be pronounced you cause
appearance to be entered on your behalf in the office of
the Court, 2 Parliament Square, Edinburgh, on the calling
of the Summons in Court, which calling will be not earlier
than the fourteenth day from the date of service upon you
of this Summons; and take warning that, if appearance is
not so entered on your behalf, the pursuer may proceed to
obtain decree against you in your absence.

The word 'divorce' is not mentioned until the details of evidence, which follow.

Some defenders take no action on receiving a summons. Some go to a solicitor for
explanation, or to question financial or custody proposals. Very few dispute the
evidence for divorce. If the defender wishes to challenge the financial or custody
arrangements or to add or alter proposals for access to children, the parties' two
solicitors usually negotiate between themselves and come to an agreement. Over the
past few years, more than 96 per cent of divorce actions have been undefended at
proof, but the number of defended divorces granted is unknown, since in a few
actions (4 per cent in 1977) divorce is refused, including some undefended actions.

Court Proceedings

In Scotland, every divorce action is heard at the Court of Session in Edinburgh.
Until May 1978 every divorce pursuer and his witness had to appear in person at
the Court of Session. The pursuer usually had a few weeks' notice of the date when
the divorce action would be heard.

Before starting on my pilot interviews in May 1977, and on several occasions
during the following twelve months, I visited the Court of Session to observe
divorce hearings. In order to gain a well-balanced impression, I sat in the courts
of eight of the twelve judges who heard most divorce actions, some of them on
several occasions.

Solicitors in four legal firms kindly gave me information about how they handled
divorce cases, so that my observations in court and my research interviews could
be placed in context.

All pursuers were instructed by their solicitors to arrive at the Court before
10 a.m. On arrival, a court official directed them to the waiting area attached to
the particular court where their case would be heard, several of thirteen courts
being used simultaneously. The pursuer's agent (often a legally unqualified member
of staff from the Edinburgh solicitor's firm) would find the pursuer and witness,
and explain what would happen in court. Some agents were punctilious about con-
tacting their clients soon after arrival. Some, knowing that their client's case
would not be heard till later in the morning, did not make contact until later,
especially if they had cases in several courts in one morning.

When a pursuer's name was called over the public address system, he was taken into
court by the agent, following the counsel who had often (but not always) had a few
words with the client in the public waiting area. The pursuer was directed by a
macer into the witness box and took the oath administered by the judge who,
wearing a wig and a red robe, was behind a raised bench with a shorthand writer
beside him. The pursuer and witness were each expected to stand while they gave
evidence. Occasionally, a judge then courteously suggested to each in turn that
they might like to sit down in the witness box, but one or two judges spoke
sharply to anyone who tentatively sat down after taking the oath. The counsel
stood in the front row of benches facing the judge, with the agent sitting behind

him. The counsel (dressed in a wig and a black gown) asked leading questions of
the pursuer, to check name, address, age, date of marriage, details of children,
and to get confirmation of the written evidence on which the case had been founded.
This was normally quick and straightforward, but could be distressing for pursuers
who were divorcing their spouses for cruelty or unreasonable behaviour. In those
cases, the questions were 'was your marriage happy?' or 'am I right in thinking
that your marriage became unhappy after a while?' followed by a request for
details. The only evidence about the welfare of children was usually given by an
affirmative answer to the question 'Are your children happy and well looked after?'
Sometimes information was requested about the number of bedrooms in a house.

After the pursuer's evidence, the witness went through the same procedure, the
witness usually being a parent or sibling (or an enquiry agent for adultery
evidence). Some judges clearly had difficulty in hearing or understanding what was
said.

At the end of the evidence, the judge gave or indicated his decision in terms of
decree granted, with details of financial awards, custody and expenses (where
applicable). Some judges were totally inaudible as they granted yet another
divorce, often doing so by a wordless nod to the counsel while the pursuer was
being led out of court by his solicitor.

The time taken for an undefended case ranged from four minutes to twenty or more;
most lasted for about seven minutes.

Evidence by Affidavit

Since 25 May 1978, there has been no need for pursuers or witnesses to attend the
vast majority of undefended divorce actions. By an Act of Sederunt of 25 January
1978 (Court of Session, 1978) evidence has been provided in writing by means of
sworn affidavits. Defended actions have continued to be heard in open court, and
also any undefended actions where a judge has ordered a hearing.

The new procedure produced unexpected delays in granting divorces, and there was
an immediate drop in the weekly number of divorces granted from 300 to 30 (Swinton
and Clark, 1978). Although some clear notes of guidance were issued to advocates
and solicitors (Dean of Faculty of Advocates, 1978) uncertainty prevailed for many
months over the content of, and the method of drafting, affidavit evidence. There
was no longer the possibility of drawing out further information in open court.
Therefore the written evidence had to be comprehensive, to cover all possible
queries from judges, some of whom were known to want more information than others
about, for instance, access by an absent parent, after-school care for children or
financial resources. So many unsatisfactory or incomplete affidavits were lodged
in the first few months of the new procedure that the Court of Session sent to the
Law Society a list of 18 'common points of difficulty giving rise to delays in
affidavit procedure' (Jnl. Law Soc. Scotland, 1979).

An undefended divorce in Scotland (in 1979) cost upward of £250 (even when there
were no children), but could cost £16, without a solicitor, in England and Wales,
where a petitioner could prepare his own petition and statement about the arrangements for children's residence, education and financial provision. Notes of
guidance are issued by the Lord Chancellor's Office for completing the various
sections on printed forms (1977). In 1980, Legal Aid is still available for
pursuers in undefended divorce actions in Scotland, (although not in England and
Wales) and expenses are normally awarded against the husband.

CHAPTER 2

METHODOLOGY

This study is a two year exploratory investigation into the sources of help, advice and support used by those going through the process of divorce in Edinburgh from July 1977 to October 1978.

My method was to use a framework of semi-structured interviews with, ideally, both spouses from 60 divorces, making 120 interviews. This was a convenient total, since it could be sub-divided into equal numbers of husband-pursuers, wife-defenders, wife-pursuers and husband-defenders.[1] Comparisons could then easily be made between husbands and wives or between pursuers and defenders in their descriptions of help received before divorce. For reasons of economy in time and expense, the sampling frame was limited to divorces where both parties had Edinburgh addresses at divorce. As in Chester's study (1975), all had, in theory, access to the same statutory and voluntary social services.

If it had proved difficult to gain a good response from defenders, as Chester (1975) had suggested, I would have hoped instead to interview 100 pursuers. To my knowledge, no previous researcher had attempted to interview both parties to divorce. Subsequently, Murch (1977) published an account of interviews with both parties in 41 divorces in south west England in which a Divorce Court welfare officer had prepared reports on the children of those divorces. This was a specialised sample, since the parents were invited by the welfare officer, whom they already knew, to participate in the research, and they were all couples from whom the court had required more information about the children. They were inter-viewed in 1973-4.

There is no public access to recent lists of divorces granted in Scotland, but names and addresses of pending divorce actions are in the Rolls of Court Calling Lists, posted daily in a public corridor of the Court of Session. These lists are therefore available to the public, although they are displayed for the convenience of solicitors and their agents. The lists are also sent daily to lawyers who subscribe to them (£75 per annum in 1977). Divorce actions can be identified in the Calling Lists as being virtually all of those cases where both parties have the same surname. Full names and addresses of both spouses are given and also the

---

[1] In Scottish legal terminology, the parties to a divorce are pursuer and defender, corresponding to petitioner and respondent in England and Wales

11

names of the counsel (advocate) and the Edinburgh solicitor for the pursuer. If the latter is legally aided, the initials AP are given after the name (Assisted Person). In the rare case of a defended action, the defender's counsel and solicitor are also named. By Scottish custom, women's surnames are given as 'A or B' where A is their maiden name and B is their married name; if they have been married more than once, all surnames may be given (A or B or C ...). If a woman's address is c/o A, that almost certainly indicates that she is living at her parents' home, and is a useful clue before an interview.

The Calling Lists give advance notice that the cases listed will be heard within, probably, two to eight weeks.

METHOD OF APPROACHING RESPONDENTS

There were two possible methods of asking divorcees for an interview, with arguments in favour of either: a written or a doorstep approach. The experiences of others who had interviewed on sensitive subjects were valuable.

An advance, written, request for interview can given the potential respondent time to understand the purpose of the research and an opportunity to think of relevant information before the interview.

Marsden (1969) wrote to 215 unsupported mothers in receipt of National Assistance. He had no direct access to names and addresses, but his letters were despatched for him by the National Assistance Board. Mothers who were prepared to be interviewed were asked to return a card in a reply paid envelope. Initially, 39 per cent agreed to be interviewed, and a further 10 per cent responded after a reminder had been sent. Marsden traced a further 7 per cent through acquaintances, and all but one of 16 mothers then approached (without a letter) agreed to be interviewed. From this mixed experience, Marsden concluded that a doorstep explanation is more likely to be understood than a written one, however carefully worded.

Elston, Fuller and Murch (1975) wrote to 145 divorce petitioners, giving a time when an interviewer would call. This produced an overall response rate of 70 per cent (21 per cent refused and 9 per cent were not traced). Of those actually contacted, 77 per cent were interviewed and 23 per cent refused.

One hazard of informing respondents by post of the research is that letters may be seen (with or without the permission of the recipient), or even opened, by other members of the household, who might then deny the interviewer access to the respondent.

A doorstep approach takes people unawares. They might then instinctively refuse to be interviewed, whereas with forethought they might have co-operated; or they might agree and subsequently regret their hasty decision. Either response might be given as the line of least resistance, and not as a considered reply.

Goode (1956) decided that he would have a high refusal rate if he forewarned divorced mothers that interviewers would call. From 710 doorstep approaches, 61 per cent were interviewed. 15 per cent refused and 24 per cent were untraced in spite of his elaborate and perhaps ethically questionable methods of tracing respondents with the assistance of the post office. Of the 537 women actually contacted, 81 per cent agreed to be interviewed and 19 per cent refused.

Chester (1975) made a doorstep approach to 324 female petitioners and interviewed 67 per cent (12 per cent refused and 21 per cent were untraced): 85 per cent of

those contacted (15 per cent refused). He did not attempt to interview divorce
respondents (i.e. defenders) because he thought they would be more likely to
refuse and that women respondents would be relatively hard to trace. He also considered that it would be difficult to interview both parties to a divorce since
the knowledge that the other was to be interviewed would probably lead to a high
refusal rate.

Cartwright and Tucker (1967) twice conducted an experiment using letters to
alternate respondents: in a pilot survey to investigate people's health and the
use of doctors, and in a study of parents of young children. In the former, where
alternate respondents were asked to return a form suggesting times for interviews,
14 per cent of those who had received letters replied that they did not wish to be
interviewed, and a further 31 per cent (who had not replied) later refused. Only
13 per cent refused of those who had had no warning of the interviewer's visit. In
the second experiment, the researchers found that the excellent response rate
among mothers was unaffected by an advance letter but that the letter halved the
refusal rate among fathers (Cartwright and Tucker, 1969). In the first survey,
advance letters had adversely affected the response but in the second, letters had
increased the response.

Whatever the approach, many people welcome an invitation to talk about themselves,
and especially about a time of crisis in their lives. The words 'research' and
'university' might flatter respondents and be important in tipping the scales in
favour of granting an interview. Other researchers had made a decision about
whether or not to forewarn respondents of an interview. The small amount of
evidence available seemed to show a slightly higher response rate from a doorstep
approach. In my own case, my appearance on the doorstep might have an additional
advantage over a written approach. Respondents who might feel doubtful about an
unknown correspondent, might be willing to talk to a middle-aged woman.

I decided to test the two methods against each other in the course of this
research. Accordingly, in the pilot study in May to July 1977, I used each
approach to each of four categories of divorce: wife-pursuer, husband-defender,
husband-pursuer and wife-defender (8 people in all). Then I also made a doorstep
approach to two husbands and two wives of those already interviewed, to gain
information from both parties to four of the eight divorces. Since there had been
only one refusal (from a doorstep approach to a wife-pursuer), I continued to use
both methods of approach alternately in the main study, in order more fully to
test each. A comparison of the results is given in Chapter 3.

PILOT STUDY

The experience gained from the twelve interviews in the pilot study, May to July
1977, was encouraging. All the respondents had been very willing to talk to me,
apart from the one refusal. Whether I had written or merely arrived on the doorstep, they all welcomed me into their homes with an air of expectancy. A few
changes were made in the introductory questions for the main sample, chiefly in
the order of questions.

My lack of knowledge of the legal procedure became apparent during the pilot
interviews, and I was grateful to several members of the legal profession who
kindly provided me with information.

Initial impressions gained from interviewing were that the third party in a
divorce for adultery did not always become a permanent new partner; arrangements
for the care of the children were taken for granted and not examined or questioned
by the parties to a divorce; there was a transitional household composition

between separation and divorce; and some partners got on better together after the
decision to end the marriage. Pursuers showed relief, triumph or a sense of
freedom. Defenders showed disbelief or were fatalistic, perhaps having dis-
regarded warnings of trouble. Both tended to suffer from loneliness.

SAMPLING FRAME

The sampling frame consisted of a series of time-clusters of all pursuers and
defenders in divorce decrees granted from July 1977 to October 1978, where both
parties had Edinburgh addresses. These time-clusters were later stratified after
interviews had been obtained with 30 wife-pursuers and then with 30 husband-
defenders, so that in the later stages of the research only husband-pursuers and
wife-defenders were required for interview.

On evidence from past Calling Lists in the Rolls of Court, it seemed likely that
in any one week there would be about fifteen divorce decrees which had two
Edinburgh addresses. With certain provisos, interviews were sought with as many
individuals as possible from a non-consecutive series of weekly lists of divorces.
The provisos were:

> (a) that interviews should take place within two months of
>   divorce, before time had clouded the memory of the pre-
>   divorce period of separation. Any bias from time-lag
>   could thus be reduced to a minimum;

> (b) that if the first spouse approached in any divorce were
>   not interviewed for any reason, the second spouse would
>   not be approached, in order to decrease the number of
>   divorces with only one party interviewed. If the first
>   to be approached were interviewed but, for whatever
>   reason, not the second, the first interview would be
>   preserved as part of the sample;

> (c) that divorces granted after more than five years'
>   separation (which, without the consent of the defender,
>   became one of the proofs of irretrievable breakdown of
>   marriage from 1 January 1977) should be excluded from
>   the sample. These marriages would have been too long
>   dead to provide information of value to the study. They
>   could not normally be identified before interview;

> (d) that I would omit any couple where one or both were
>   known to me. (In the event, none were known).

My original sampling proposal, to seek to interview three times as many wife-
pursuers as husband-pursuers, to conform with the previous overall Scottish
pattern, was changed to give equal numbers of each, because there might be
different behaviour patterns of pursuers and of defenders, and thirty interviews
in each of four categories was probably the least number which could yield useful
information.

There was, in any case, no known pattern of Edinburgh divorces, since the
published statistics are for the whole of Scotland, and even the 1977 Scottish
pattern under the Divorce (Scotland) Act 1976 might well be different from the
previous pattern.

The pursuer had no control over the date of a divorce hearing. The Assistant Keeper

of Rolls allocated cases from all over Scotland to days and to judges. When cases
were heard in court, he normally collected together several divorces with the same
counsel, although these may have had different Edinburgh solicitors. Consequently,
a series of time-clusters of Edinburgh divorces should have a reasonable chance of
being representative of the divorcing Edinburgh population. Goode said, of his
four time-clusters of divorced mothers drawn from the complete records in one
county court, 'A sample drawn from this list can be considered random if it
follows a defensible sampling plan' (Goode, 1956).

Contested Divorces

In 1977 only 3.6 per cent of all Scottish divorce actions (granted or refused)
were defended at proof (Civil Judicial Statistics, Scotland, 1977). This included
6.5 per cent of actions heard under the old legislation and 0.85 per cent of those
under the new. It was unlikely that more than one or two defended divorces would
be within my sample of 120 interviews (a minimum of 60 divorces). Clive found that
in his 1975 Scottish sample, defences had been lodged in 10 per cent of divorces
where there were children under 16 (Eekelaar and Clive, 1977, para 9.9). He had
earlier described those cases as 'semi-defended' (Clive and Wilson, 1974).
Probably some such cases would occur in my sample, but during the fieldwork it
became clear that many respondents did not know much about legal negotiations over
their divorce and did not know whether defences had been lodged.

FIELDWORK

Divorced couples were numbered and were allocated alternately to letter/doorstep
or doorstep/letter approach. Each address was then marked on a clean sheet of
paper which was, in effect, a blank map of Edinburgh with three landmarks shown –
Princes Street, the university and my home. Pursuers' numbers were entered in
black and defenders' in red, each with the letter L for letter or D for doorstep.
This gave the geographical scatter of people to be interviewed. It was possible,
especially with the early, longer, lists of about fifteen couples, to plan a
group of calls in one area of the city.

Difficulties Encountered

A difficulty arose soon after starting to interview the main sample, in attempting
to see first equal numbers of pursuers and of defenders. Defenders are not
informed that they have been divorced until three weeks after the event. In theory,
this is to allow them time to appeal against the decision but in practice, since
they often do not even know the date of the divorce hearing, they clearly cannot
appeal. This practice may have made sense at a time when both parties had to
attend court, but it appears to have become meaningless. (An additional problem
could be created for defenders, who know that divorce actions have been raised
against them through service of a summons, but who might never know if the
pursuers had dropped their actions). A result of this practice was that I could
not interview defenders until at least three weeks after the divorce, by which
time half of the target interview period of two months was nearly over. Therefore
the attempt was abandoned to interview equal numbers of pursuers and defenders
first. Unfortunately this resulted in more wife-pursuers than husband-defenders
being approached first, so that the target for thirty wife-pursuers was completed
before that for husband-defenders, four of whom had to be interviewed with no
possibility of their wives being part of the sample. However, the importance of
this is small.

After evidence by affidavit was introduced in May 1978, pursuers did not know of
their divorce until they were informed by their solicitors, and it was safer for
me not to approach either party until the expiry of the three week period.

Sixty-six of the 223 individuals whom I contacted were no longer at the address
given, which was often the address supplied by the pursuer when starting divorce
proceedings. Many were traced to their new addresses and twenty-six were interviewed after information had been given by relatives or neighbours, or by other
tracing procedures including the old and current voters' rolls, or by clues
picked up in an interview with the spouse. One wife (whose husband's new address
neither she nor I knew) had mentioned the name of the church he attended, and
that his parents lived near that church. The telephone directory yielded three
entries of that surname in the same district as the church. The marriage had been
ten years back, and reference to the voters' roll of eleven years back revealed a
man of the name required at one of the three possible addresses. A visit to that
address resulted in the current address being given to me by the man's father.
However, the street was a new one and even the Regional Assessor's office knew
the district but not the exact location. The police finally gave directions for
finding the street, and the man was interviewed. Perseverance was rewarded.

Three potential respondents denied being divorced. One was a wife-defender who was
no longer at her original address. I had traced her and had called on her four and
a half weeks after the divorce decree, which should have reached her after three
weeks. She told me that her divorce had not yet been granted and that she would
prefer not to talk about it. Another was a man, whose new address was given to me
by the new occupier of his previous flat. The man I subsequently found answered to
the correct first name and surname, but told me that his wife had died some years
previously. We discovered that the second and third Christian names which I had
were those of this man's son, while the first was the man's (but not his son's).
This man had never heard of the address where I had first called. Probably the son
had lived there after his marriage had ended, but without telling his father, whom
he visited regularly, ostensibly after driving his wife to another destination.
The father had had a suspicion that all was not well with the marriage, had understood me to say a divorce was pending and waved aside my apologies. I left my
phone number, and a few days later the son telephoned me and was very pleasant: he
had not previously told his father about his marital breakdown but had now done
so. Since he had moved to live outside Edinburgh, he was outwith my sample, and I
did not ask to interview him.

Although all potential respondents had Edinburgh addresses, fieldwork could be
frustratingly time-consuming. A call at a given address could lead to a new
address in a different area of town; to the information that the respondent was at
work (and possibly on a different shift the next day) or visiting relatives; or to
a request to return at a more convenient time (possibly only to discover that the
marital separation had been for more than five years). If there were no reply and
also no information from neighbours, it was necessary to decide whether to wait
nearby and to return a little later or whether to return on another day. My
respondent might have been out of the house for a few minutes only, for several
hours or even on holiday. Some of these difficulties could have been overcome by
offering, or asking for, an appointment, but there might have been a poor response
to such an approach.

Two wives were interviewed beyond the time limit of two months after divorce
because of difficulties in tracing them. Also, four husbands and six wives were
interviewed up to three months after divorce because the scarcity of divorces
granted in the summer and early autumn of 1978 necessitated the inclusion in the
sample of earlier divorces from weeks which had previously been omitted. It seemed
unlikely that the slightly longer time that had elapsed since divorce would have

had much, if any, effect on these respondents' memories or accounts of events after separation.

The Interview

On arrival at an address, I asked for the respondent by name, having no idea of what age to expect. Whoever came to the door might be the potential respondent or his parent or his child or even a stranger. If the respondent were not at home, I asked when he would be in. Sometimes this information was freely given, sometimes the purpose of my visit was requested, in which case my answer was that I wanted to interview the named person for some research. No details were given to satisfy the curiosity of relatives. If the respondent had already had my letter explaining the research, there was occasionally a proxy refusal at this point (the truth of which could not be tested), such as 'he had your letter and he is definitely not interested'.

Having found the person sought, it was necessary either to give my name (to those who had had a letter [1]) or to introduce myself and to give the same explanation as others had had in writing.

Many respondents (and, indeed, many relatives) invited me in most warmly without waiting for the whole introduction, which then had to be completed inside the house. I had expected the word 'divorce' to cause some people to flinch, but few batted an eyelid. Some listened politely until the word 'divorce' was reached, at which point they showed enthusiasm and a positive willingness to co-operate. It seemed that many of those divorced were flattered to be asked about their experiences, and were not concerned about the purpose of the research. None assumed (except for one wife, ineligible for inclusion in the sample because she had been too long separated), as some of Bott's respondents had initially done, that they were being offered a form of social work (Bott, 1957). Some asked at the close of the interview, for the explanation to be repeated. A few suggested that I return to monitor progress.

Each interview started with a few simple questions, partly to set the respondent at ease and partly to set the rest of the interview in context: age and occupation of both spouses, dates of marriage, separation and divorce, age and sex of any children of the marriage, proximity of parental home at time of marriage and of separation, whether parents had approved the marriage, number of siblings and whether the divorce had been legally aided. I already knew whether the respondent had been pursuer or defender.

Next, I asked 'was there anyone in particular you turned to for help?' 'Anyone you talked to?' was added if the first question brought no response.

---

[1] I am writing to ask for your assistance in some research being done in the University. We are told that people face a lot of difficulties in finding the right kind of personal help and advice before divorce. Your name was on a list of divorces granted recently, and I would very much like to ask you about your experiences. You would not be asked any personal questions about your marriage, but only about the kind of help you may have had, and your opinions about that help.

I will call to see you in a few days, and look forward to meeting you. Anything that you tell me will, of course, be completely confidential. (Letters were individually typed, so that they did not look like circulars).

The direction of the rest of the interview was determined by information freely given by the respondent and then in response to probes or prompts, in which I picked up references made by the respondent. I finally glanced through a check list of possible sources of help (formal or informal) and of possible areas in which help might have been needed (see Appendix 1).

It was not possible to know in advance whether the respondent would find the subject of his divorce sensitive, absorbing, boring or fascinating; or whether he would want to pour out his story, bottle it up, submit to questioning with an ill-grace or with eagerness.

The advantages of using a framework for a semi-structured interview were that it allowed the respondent to define the situation and to put his own spontaneous interpretation on the key word 'help'. It was equally possible to keep the respondent's interest without asking questions which appeared irrelevant to him or which distracted from his line of thought. Unstructured refers to the shape and order of the interview rather than to the overall content (Cohen and Taylor, 1977).

Benney and Hughes (1956) wrote that the more freely information is given, the more valid it is: that it is satisfying to the respondent to give information which is not challenged or contradicted. Merton and Kendall (1956) used the term 'focused' interview, which they defined as determining the responses of persons exposed to a situation previously defined by the investigator, with the minimum of guidance from the interviewer. They considered that a focused interview would yield far more information than one directed by an interviewer. Further, Merton, Fiske and Kendall (1956) pointed out that a focused interview encourages self-exploration, provides for spontaneity, makes unanticipated responses possible and 'ordinarily leads the interviewee to be more articulate and expressive than in the directed interview'. They recommended the interviewer to encourage retrospection, to use an interview guide, to 'ferret out meanings' and to differentiate between casual opinion offered because it was requested and a genuine opinion of importance to the respondent. Similarly, Becker and Geer (1960) emphasised that information offered voluntarily may be more valuable than that given in response to questioning.

My main concern was to enquire about sources of help (practical, emotional or professional) used between separation and divorce, opinions about the help sought or offered, given or refused, and reasons for using any particular agency or individual. I had at first intended to gain information about the factors leading to marital breakdown, in order to put into context any help received, but I soon abandoned this idea as being too sensitive and partly irrelevant. It would have meant starting an interview with questions about the marriage, and might have prejudiced chances of success in the later part of an interview. Additionally, pre-separation marital problems would not necessarily influence post-separation problems. These were two different areas to be explored, and it was better to concentrate on one. However, some useful information was offered and recorded about help-seeking prior to separation.

There was a sharp contrast between this kind of interviewing and my previous experience as a marriage counsellor. In both, the course of the interview could be guided by the respondent (client), but now it was my task to draw out as much information as possible for my own ends, rather than concentrating on the client's needs.

Tape-recording was judged to be inhibiting to respondents, time-consuming to transcribe and possibly unreliable, and I had had no experience. Memory would not provide comprehensive recall of interviews. It remained to take full notes in a form of abbreviated longhand, taking down verbatim anything which was particularly interesting. Time could be gained where necessary, by repeating words as they were written. It was important to maintain rapport by pausing, and looking at the respondent frequently, especially to see facial expressions or gestures. Each interview was typed, within 24 hours, as a narrative averaging 2500 words.

If someone else were present at the start of the interview and did not melt away tactfully, it was necessary either to ask the respondent whether he would prefer to talk in private, or to decide not to risk antagonising anyone by suggesting that the presence of their friend or relative might be resented by me. The former course never caused any withdrawals by respondents or by interested listeners. The latter course may have resulted in accounts which were not completely frank, but may also have made the difference between the respondent agreeing to an interview or refusing. It seemed preferable to interview with another person present rather than to risk a refusal. Those present at interview included 17 new partners (nearly half of the total number of new partners), a parent on ten occasions and a sibling on five. On some occasions, further information was added in confidence on the doorstep as I was leaving.

It was interesting that almost all respondents looked on themselves as individuals, and not as halves of a divorce. Only two asked whether I would be interviewing their ex-spouse and one of these, a wife-defender, did not wait for a reply but said 'do excuse me while I feed the dog'. The other, a husband-pursuer, was quite willing for me to see his ex-wife, but said that he would tell her not to give me any personal information.

The length of interviews averaged 45 minutes, with a range of 15 minutes (both halves of one couple who appeared to have taken separation in their stride and still met frequently) to $2\frac{1}{2}$ hours. A method was devised to demonstrate the running total of interviews completed (giving here the position after 59 interviews):

PURSUERS						DEFENDERS					
Husbands			Wives			Husbands			Wives		
C	F	U	A	J	K	B	E	H	T	AB	
AG			L	O	P	I	M	N			
			Q	AC	AD	R	V	W			
			AE	AF	AH	Z					

Each small square was marked with a divorce reference letter, to show in how many divorces interviews had been obtained with both spouses

Letter

G	T	Y	B	D	E	K	O	Q	C	F	U
AB			H	I	M	AA	AC	AD	AG		
			N	R	S	AE	AF	AH			
			V	W	X	AI					
			Z								

Doorstep

CHAPTER 3

THE SAMPLE

The target of 120 interviews took sixteen months to complete, July 1977 to
November 1978. Respondents were equally divided between husband-pursuer, wife-
defender, wife-pursuer and husband-defender to facilitate comparisons and to gain
sufficient information about each. Attempts were made to contact 227 individuals
on the sampling frame and 507 calls were made at their addresses, with the
following results:

TABLE 3.1   Results of Attempts to Interview

	Husband pursuer	Wife defender	Wife pursuer	Husband defender	Total
Interviewed	30	30	30	30	120
Refused	5	8	3	6	22
Gone away, untraced	7	4	4	9	24
Never at home	3	2	–	6	11
Left Edinburgh	4	5	2	5	16
Separated over 5 years	15	13	2	4	34
Individuals	64	62	41	60	227

Excluding those who were discovered to have left Edinburgh or who had been
separated for over five years, 68 per cent were interviewed, 12 per cent refused
and 20 per cent were not traced. Of those who were traced (and living in
Edinburgh, with a marital separation of less than five years), 85 per cent were
interviewed and 15 per cent refused.

Both parties were interviewed in each of 43 divorces and one in each of 34
divorces (eight each of husband-pursuers and wife-defenders; nine each of wife-
pursuers and husband-defenders).

Interviews were most often obtained after one or two calls, but others required up
to six calls. At least three, and a mean of five, calls were made before a

potential respondent was abandoned and classified as 'never at home'.

CHARACTERISTICS OF THE SAMPLE

There are no known statistics relating to Edinburgh domiciled divorces, so it was not possible to compare the characteristics of the sample with those of the divorcing population of Edinburgh. However, some comparisons can be made with the divorcing population of Scotland and with the adult male population of Edinburgh.

Pursuers were equally divided between husbands and wives in the sample, but in all Scottish divorces granted in 1977, pursuers were wives in 75 per cent (Civil Judicial Statistics, Scotland, 1977). This discrepancy was intentional. It might be necessary to adjust the findings if it were required to relate them to the Scottish population.

Age at Marriage

The ages at marriage of the husbands and wives in the sample of 77 divorces were very similar to those in all Scottish divorces in 1977, the last year for which published figures were available when this was written, and also the year in which 35 per cent of the divorces in the sample were granted.

TABLE 3.2   Comparison of Age at Marriage between Sample
              and all Scottish Divorces in 1977

Age at marriage	Husbands %		Wives %	
	Sample	All Scottish	Sample	All Scottish
16 – 18	10	10	23	29
19 – 20	18	21	26	29
21 – 24	42	42	34	28
25 – 29	21	18	14	8
30 and over	9	9	3	6
	(n=77)	(n=8540)	(n=77)	(n=8540)

Source: Registrar General Scotland : Annual report for 1977, Tables R2.6.1 and R2.6.2

The discrepancy between the total number of divorces in 1977 reported by the Registrar General (8540) and in the Civil Judicial Statistics (8812) is caused by the exclusion from the Registrar General's figures of people who were divorced under pre-1976 legislation and who had not been married in Scotland.

Age at Divorce

Husbands and wives in the sample tended to be younger than those in all Scottish divorces in 1977. A far higher proportion of husbands and of wives in the sample than in Scotland had divorced before the age of 34 and, in particular, a higher proportion of husbands before the age of 24. A probable explanation is that the sample excluded divorces granted after a separation of five years or more which, without the consent of the defender, became a ground for divorce in 1977: such divorces were likely to be of older couples.

TABLE 3.3   Comparison of Age at Divorce between Sample
and all Scottish Divorces in 1977

Age at divorce	Husbands %		Wives %	
	Sample	All Scottish	Sample	All Scottish
Up to 24	19	13	23	21
25 – 29	22	23	29	24
30 – 34	29	18	27	16
35 and over	30	46	21	39
	(n=77)	(n=8540	(n=77)	(n=8540)

Source: Registrar General Scotland : Annual report for 1977, Part 2,
        Tables R2.5.1 and R2.5.2

Length of Marriage

Official statistics give only the de jure length of marriage (i.e. the legal
marriage to the date of divorce). The mean de jure length of the sample marriages
was 9 years and for Scottish marriages divorced in 1977 was 12.8 years, including
those divorced after more than five years' separation (Registrar General for
Scotland (RGS) : Annual report for 1977, Part 2, p.21).

To a certain extent, the de jure length of marriage is an arbitrary one, since the
parties cannot determine the exact date of termination of the marriage. More
important, it includes the time of separation before divorce, when the marriage is
legally in existence but not physically so. Respondents were therefore asked the
date of separation, so that the de facto length of marriage (before the couple had
separated) could be measured.

The mean de facto length of the 77 marriages was just under seven years, ranging
from two weeks to 21 years. For the childless couples the mean was four years, but
this included many of the shortest de facto marriages. For six couples (8 per cent)
the de facto marriage had lasted for one year or less; for one quarter of the
sample it had lasted for two years or less, and for one half of the sample for
four years or less. Chester (1975) found that separations reached their peak in
the third year of marriage. Marginally more in this sample had separated in the
second year of marriage than in the third.

According to official statistics, only 2 per cent of marriages ended by divorce in
1977 had lasted for two years or less (Civil Judicial Statistics, Scotland, 1977)
and 20 per cent for 4 years or less (RGS for 1977, Table R1.4). These figures
disguise the fact that many marriages break up within two years.

The length of time between separation and divorce varied, for the sample, from ten
days to 4¼ years. Nearly half had had a separation of two years or less.

Grounds for Divorce

The sole ground for divorce since 1 January 1977 has been the irretrievable breakdown of marriage, but the evidence required for such breakdown is very similar to the previous grounds for divorce. Most of those in the sampling-frame had been divorced under the new legislation, but a few of those interviewed at the beginning of the research probably gained their divorces under the old legislation. It was obvious that some did not know the difference. Therefore, for convenience, grounds for divorce were listed as adultery, unreasonable behaviour (or cruelty), desertion, and separation (for two years, with the defender's consent to divorce).

For comparison with official statistics of divorces, divorces granted after five years' separation are included, although they were not eligible for inclusion in the sample, and were removed from the sampling-frame after identification.

TABLE 3.4   Grounds for Divorce Compared with all Scottish
             Divorces in 1977 and 1978 under New Legislation

	Adultery	Unreasonable behaviour	Desertion	2 years separation	5 years separation
contacted % (n=111) [1]	14	24	4	27	31
divorces granted in Scotland in 1977, new legislation % (n=4707)	20	37	9	12	22
divorces granted in Scotland in 1978, new legislation % (n=7950)	17	36	5	20	22

[1] Includes 34 divorces in the sampling-frame which were found to be ineligible for this sample after being contacted, because of separations of more than five years.

Figures were not published until January 1980 for Scottish divorces granted in 1978 (Civil Judicial Statistics, Scotland, 1978). This was too late for comparison with the research divorces, of which 65 per cent had been granted in 1978. The main difference between the two years was likely to be seen in the new grounds, which would have become better established by 1978. Therefore Scottish figures have been included in this Table only for both years, showing a swing from adultery and desertion to two years' separation in 1978.

The figures for those contacted are different in some respects from the 1977 and 1978 national figures, but the effect of the new legislation was only beginning to be seen. Respondents living in a city might have been quick to take advantage of the new grounds for divorce. Although a solicitor would probably prefer more concrete evidence of breakdown than the written consent of a defender who might change his mind, some pursuers interviewed had chosen to wait for two years for a divorce by consent, rather than to use other available grounds. Additionally, some of those rejected from the sampling-frame because of separations of more than five years, might not have used that as a ground for divorce.

Social Class

It was convenient to categorise respondents by the social classes used by the
Registrar General for Scotland, namely: I (professional), II (executive and
managerial), IIIN (skilled non-manual), IIIM (skilled manual), IV (partly skilled)
and V (unskilled) (OPCS, 1970). Other kinds of division are less well known and
more complicated. The Registrar General's social class divisions are used for
censuses and official statistics, and can be used for comparison. For this study,
both spouses were allocated to social class according to the husband's occupation.

The media give publicity to divorces within social classes I and II because these
are of interest to the public. There is little news value in run-of-the-mill
divorces of manual workers living in local authority housing. This factor can lead
to the myth that divorce is an upper middle-class phenomenon.

Rowntree and Carrier (1958) found that in 1951 the divorcing and the still married
had similar occupational distribution. Gibson (1974) found that the only classes
with a percentage of divorces granted in 1961 higher than that of the still
married were class IIIN (19 per cent of all divorces; 13 per cent of all still
married) and class V (11 per cent and 8 per cent); these being, respectively, the
lowest of the non-manual and of the manual classes. He showed also that the
numbers of divorces granted in 1961 per thousand married women under the age of 55
was highest in those two classes (43 in IIIN and 51 in V), and lowest in class I
(22). Gibson suggested that the explanation may have lain in the fact that manual
workers marry younger than non-manual and that early marriage leads to divorce:
the link between young marriages, social class and divorce may have been financial.

There are no official figures about the social class of divorces of Edinburgh
residents, nor of Scottish divorces. The sample can be compared only with the
social class of the total adult male population of Edinburgh in 1971.

TABLE 3.5   Social Class of Sample and of Edinburgh Adult
             Males in 1971

	I	II	IIIN	IIIM	IV	V
Sample % (n=77)	6	16	12	35	22	9
All Edinburgh males aged 15+ in 1971 %	9	17	14	35	16	9

Source: Census of Scotland 1971. Economic activity Part II (10% sample). The
        social class distribution of married males in Edinburgh is not given

This indicates that social class I may have the lowest divorce rate in Edinburgh
and social class IV the highest.

Children

In all Scottish divorce actions in 1977, 65 per cent had children under 16 (and
thus under the jurisdiction of the court). In the sample, 62 per cent of the 77
divorces had children under 16.

The proportion of couples with children under 16 increased the lower the social
class, with the exception of social class IIIN where this proportion was lower
than in II or IIIM.

Childlessness was not simply associated with short marriages: those in class IIIM (37 per cent childless) had the shortest marriages and classes I and IV had the longest (80 per cent and 17 per cent childless respectively).

In the 48 divorces in the sample where there were children under 16, the children lived with ten fathers (all pursuers) and 38 mothers (28 pursuers and 10 defenders). Therefore in 21 per cent the children were with fathers and in 79 per cent with mothers. In all, 86 children under 16 were involved.

These ten fathers were all interviewed, as were 31 of the 38 mothers. Four of these ten fathers and seven of the 31 mothers had new partners. Therefore children in at least eleven (i.e. about one quarter) of the families had already acquired substitute parents. There are no official statistics about the residence of children at the time of their parents' divorce.

WRITTEN OR DOORSTEP APPROACH

Table 3.1 showed that the 22 who refused to be interviewed represented 12 per cent of the sampling-frame, or 15 per cent of those actually contacted, while a further 35 (20 per cent) of the sampling-frame were either not traced or never at home.

The figures must be examined in the context of the experiment to test two methods of requesting an interview, the written and the doorstep approach.

TABLE 3.6   Comparison of Two Methods of Approach to Obtain
                        Interviews

Result	Method of approach		Total
	written	doorstep	
Interviewed	60	60	120
Refused	18	4	22

$$x^2 = 6.37 \text{ df } 1 \quad p < 0.01$$

Gone away, address unknown	12	12	24
Never at home (mean, 5 visits)	7	4	11
Left Edinburgh	8	8	16
Separated over 5 years [1]	13	17	30
Total	118	105	223

[1] Four others were eliminated after being found, from old voters' rolls, to have been separated for over five years.

The results showed a significantly better response from those contacted by a doorstep approach, 94 per cent being interviewed. The written approach produced a 77 per cent success rate. The seven who were never at home and who had received letters (but not appointments) had conceivably contrived not to be at home on my successive visits. While that seemed unlikely, such a reaction would have indicated an even higher refusal rate from a written approach.

The 60 interviews obtained from a written approach resulted from 136 visits; the 60 from a doorstep approach from 133 visits. Neither method was more time-consuming than the other.

Refusals

Those who refused to be interviewed were equally divided between husbands and
wives (11 of each) but 14 defenders refused compared with 8 pursuers.

One of the four who refused on the doorstep asserted that she was 'not yet
divorced' and it was indeed possible that her extract decree had not reached her
at her new address. Two of the others were initially willing to be interviewed,
but at a time more convenient to them. In the interval, one learned from his
solicitor that the research was not, as he had mistakenly assumed, a necessary
consequence to his divorce; the other had been unable to keep an appointment at
the time he had suggested and by the third call he had lost interest or patience.
It was possible that these three would have given interviews if the circumstances
had been more favourable.

Six of the eighteen who refused an interview after receiving a letter, telephoned
to refuse. Only one of the six, a wife-defender, expressed annoyance at being
approached and, according to her husband who had custody of their only child, this
had been her third marriage. Another told me on the telephone that it would be
'mutually advantageous for us to meet' and that she would later suggest a time for
interview. This woman visited her children and her divorced husband almost daily
and there learned that I had already interviewed the latter. She changed her mind
and refused to meet me but gave further information on the telephone.

Nine of those who had had letters, mainly women, refused when I subsequently
called at their homes (although some of them gave some information on the doorstep); and in the other three refusals a new partner, a mother and a son refused
access. Yet another had telephoned in my absence to leave a message that she did
not want to be interviewed. Being uncertain whether this was a definite refusal,
I ventured to call on her, to find that she had not wanted to see me, but since I
had arrived she invited me in and willingly gave an hour and a half's interview.
('But you were so nice', she explained at the end).

Response Comparison between Husbands and Wives, and between Pursuers and Defenders

Examining the difference first between the spouses and second between the parties
to divorce, it can be seen that wives and defenders were significantly more
likely to refuse a written request for interview than a doorstep request. For
husbands and for pursuers there was no significant difference in the success rate
of the two approaches.

TABLE 3.7 Effect of Two Approaches on Husbands and on Wives

| Result | HUSBANDS | | WIVES | |
| | Method of approach | | Method of approach | |
	written	doorstep	written	doorstep
Interviewed	30	30	30	30
Refused	8	3	10	1
Interviews, % of contacts	79	91	75	97

not statistically significant   1 degree of freedom $X^2 = 4.79$ p <0.05

TABLE 3.8 Effect of Two Approaches on Pursuers and on Defenders

| Result | PURSUERS | | DEFENDERS | |
| | Method of approach | | Method of approach | |
	written	doorstep	written	doorstep
Interviewed	30	30	30	30
Refused	6	2	12	2
Interviews, % of contacts	83	94	71	94

not statistically significant   1 degree of freedom $X^2 = 4.53$ p <0.05

Finally, breaking down the results still further, it can be seen that the highest refusal rate came from wife-defenders approached by letter.

TABLE 3.9 Effect of Two Approaches on Husbands and on Wives, as Pursuers and as Defenders

| Respondent | WRITTEN | | DOORSTEP | |
	Interviewed	Refused	Interviewed	Refused
Husband-pursuer	15	3	15	2
Wife-defender	15	7	15	1
Wife-pursuer	15	3	15	-
Husband-defender	15	5	15	1

Conclusions about Method of Approaching Respondents

I preferred to 'sell' my research in person rather than by post, since it was then possible to gauge reactions, to know at least the age group of the respondent, and to break the ice conversationally. On the other hand, having gained access, I knew that those to whom I had written had had an opportunity to consider the purpose of the research, and to make a conscious decision to agree to be interviewed. The doorstep acceptances might appear to have listened to my explanation, but some-times seemed to be willing to talk to any caller on any subject, and sometimes had reacted favourably to the word 'divorce' without listening carefully to the rest of the introduction. Quite a number of them asked me to repeat the purpose of the research or 'survey' as I was leaving. Some of those who agreed, after a doorstep approach, to be interviewed, might have refused a written request.

The best method for seeking interviews with a divorced population would seem to be a doorstep request.

CHAPTER 4

THE ANALYSIS

The fieldwork provided 120 narrative accounts of experiences of receiving help
mainly in the period of marital separation before divorce. They were each written
in the personal context of the interview with the respondent.

Analysis of the reports of help received was carried out in two ways. First, for
every informant, every potential source of help was coded as being of professional,
emotional or practical help, neutral, unhelpful (or a combination of these), not
approached or not applicable (i.e. the respondent had, for instance, no mother or
no colleague). The data were combined with personal details of each individual,
transferred to the computer and analysed by means of SCSS.[1] The advantages of SCSS
over the more conventional SPSS were that it not only provided instant tables and
statistics, but it allowed for experimentation by regrouping data in a search for
interesting relationships between variables. SCSS gave flexibility and avoided
delays which can be frustrating for an inexperienced user of SPSS, since any
errors could be seen immediately and corrected. These advantages outweighed any
disadvantage of occasional long pauses when a large number of people were using the
system, and results were slow to be printed. Secondly, and simultaneously, a
descriptive analysis was built up by drawing out the threads of the interviews, in
order to examine the total experience of the sample of each formal and informal
source of help in turn.

The data were unlikely to have been complete, since they included only what seemed
relevant to both the respondents and to me. However, all respondents were interviewed in a comparable way and therefore comparison between them is possible and a
description of their experiences can give an approximation to their overall views
of the help they received when their marriages broke down.

It is useful to examine first the totals used of all sources of help: emotional,
practical and professional.

This gives an average of six sources of help for each respondent, including legal
advice. Apart from lawyers, it is obvious that informal social networks were of key

---

[1] SCSS is a 'conversational' or interactive package developed by the creators of
the Statistical Package for the Social Sciences (SPSS); the user communicates
directly with the computer through a terminal

TABLE 4.1   Percentage of Sample Helped by Each Source and
by Each Available Source

% of sample helped by		% helped where sources available [1]	
Lawyers	77	New partners	82
Mothers	63	Mothers	78
Fathers	42	Lawyers	77
Friends	41	Fathers	63
Colleagues	37	Sisters	45
Doctors	34	Children	45
Children	28	Colleagues	44
Sisters	27	Friends	41
Spouses	27	Doctors	34
New partners	26	Brothers	31
Neighbours	25	Spouses	27
Brothers	19	Neighbours	25
Citizens Advice Bureau	17	Citizens Advice Bureau	17
Social workers	12	Social workers	12
Nurseries	12	Clergy	7
Mothers-in-law	11	Psychiatrists	6
Cousins, aunts etc.	11	Marriage counsellors	5
Department of Health and Social Security	10		
Housing Department	8		
Siblings' spouse	8		
Clergy	7		
Spouse's sibling	7		
Psychiatrists	6		
Marriage counsellors	5		
Miscellaneous	35		

[1] This half of the table takes account of the fact that some respondents had, for instance, no new partners, mothers, sisters or colleagues, but it assumes that all had equal access to the professions, to voluntary organisations and to friends and neighbours.

importance. Since these networks gave practical help as well as emotional support, it is now useful to isolate those who appear to have given emotional support and to compare the patterns of sources of such support used by men and by women.

While mothers and new partners were most frequently helpful, when available, there were other sources which were often mentioned and there was no one relationship offering a monopoly of care-giving. Wives differed from husbands in finding sisters and colleagues more helpful than children, friends and fathers. It is interesting to compare sources of informal emotional support with those of specialised help, and to see that only general practitioners were much used (and more often by wives than by husbands).

TABLE 4.2   Percentage of Sample with Informal Emotional
            Support by Each Source and of Sample, of
            Husbands and of Wives by Each Available Source

Source of informal emotional support	% of sample helped	Source of informal emotional support	% helped where source was available [1]		
			Whole sample	Husbands	Wives
Mothers	43	New partners	79	87	67
Friends	35	Mothers	54	45	62
Colleagues	27	Children	42	43	41
Children	27	Friends	35	32	38
New partners	25	Fathers	32	26	37
Fathers	21	Colleagues	32	24	42
Sisters	19	Sisters	31	18	46
Brothers	12	Brothers	20	16	24
Neighbours	12	Neighbours	12	10	13
Spouses	10	Spouses	10	10	10
Others [2]	30	Mothers-in-law	7	6	9
Source of specialised help (for comparison)		Source of specialised help (for comparison)			
Doctors	34	Doctors	34	17	52
Social workers	12	Social workers	12	8	17
Clergy	7	Clergy	7	5	8
Marriage counsellors	5	Marriage counsellors	5	8	2

[1] This half of the table takes account of the fact that some respondents had no
mothers, colleagues etc.

[2] 'Others' includes mothers-in-law (6 per cent), spouse's siblings, other
relatives.

The total number of sources of informal emotional support gives a mean of 2.6
sources per respondent (2.3 for husbands and 2.9 for wives).

These figures do not give any indication of the number of individual people who
gave informal emotional support to respondents, but only of the categories of
sources of support. In some categories (children, friends, colleagues, sisters,
brothers and neighbours) more than one individual might have been supportive. A
respondent might have found support from, say, several friends and not turned to
parents, or from several siblings and not turned to friends or colleagues.

Information about the numbers of individuals providing support is in the interview
narratives, but was not extracted at the time that these narratives were coded for
computer analysis. Possibly this is a fault in the coding design, but the aim had
been specifically to examine the number of sources of help used, rather than the
number of individuals.

The number of sources of informal emotional support used by respondents ranged
from nil (six husbands and one wife) to eight (one wife). Half of the sample
claimed to have used only one or two sources. Those with children appeared to have

had less support than those without. In particular, both husbands and wives who
had custody of their children had used slightly less than the mean number of
sources (2.5) while husbands who had children but not custody had used a mean of
only 1.8 sources of support. By contrast, childless husbands had used slightly
more than the mean (2.7) and childless wives had used much more (3.6). The higher
the social class, the more sources of informal support were used (but the higher
the social class, the more likely were respondents to be childless). Age at
divorce, de facto length of marriage and length of separation had had no effect on
the number of informal supports, with one important exception. Eight respondents
had had de facto marriages lasting for less than one year; they described a great
need to talk and had used a mean of four sources of informal emotional support.
Many of them had been shattered by such a speedy disillusionment about marriage,
although all except for one couple had known their partners for several years
before marriage.

Six husbands and one wife described no informal emotional support at all; three
had agreed with their spouses to end the marriage. The one wife, after a fortnight
of marriage to a long-standing boy-friend had happily returned to her large family
of origin - there had been no pre-marital pregnancy by way of explanation. Only
one man had felt let down by having no emotional support: he said, ruefully, that
his doctor's advice had been too directive to be acceptable. This man was the only
respondent to have consulted his doctor among those with no informal emotional
support. The 30 who had used only one informal source of emotional support were 17
husbands and 13 wives.

No evidence was collected to measure the depth or the continuity of sources of
support. No quantitative measures were used during the interviews. Respondents
were not asked to measure any help or support on a scale. While this might have
been a useful device, it would have interrupted the flow of interviews and provided a poorer descriptive analysis. No differentiation is made between isolated
instances of 'help' and on-going 'help' since there were too many variations. It
may well have been that some respondents found all the support they needed from
one person, and that others felt the need to talk to several people either
consecutively or concurrently. A search for such quantitative information would
have altered the focus of the interviews and might have inhibited respondents from
speaking as freely as many of them did.

No attempt was made to determine which had been the greatest source of help for
respondents. Some indication of the most important provider of support for each
of them was perhaps given by their initial replies to the question 'was there
anyone in particular you turned to for help when your marriage broke down?'
Parents (and especially mothers) were most often mentioned first. No distinction
between either of 'my parents' was made by 17 respondents. A further 19 cited their
mother first and five their father, giving a total of 41 (34 per cent) who
instinctively thought of one parent or both. These were almost equally divided
between husbands and wives.

The only other relatives whose help was given much weight at this point were
sisters, who were mentioned first by six respondents and second by three. Other
informal sources of help which first sprang to mind were nine friends (with
another six mentioned second), three neighbours and three colleagues.

Fifteen respondents mentioned their lawyer first and a further four mentioned him
second. Four referred first to social workers and three to general practitioners
(and another three referred to them second). No other source of help, either
informal or professional, was mentioned first more than three times.

CHAPTER 5

THE PROFESSIONS

LAWYERS

Throughout the period of this research, all pursuers in divorce actions in Scotland had to use the professional services of an Edinburgh solicitor (and also a local solicitor if the pursuer lived elsewhere in Scotland) and an advocate.

Defenders had no obligation to consult a solicitor unless they wished to defend the divorce itself or to dispute the proposed arrangements for their children or the financial provisions. In practice, many defenders consult a solicitor with a request to vary the proposed arrangements, or for clarification of, or information about, the process and consequences of divorce. It is rare for a defender to refute the allegations of a matrimonial offence or of irretrievable breakdown of the marriage.

TABLE 5.1   Finding a Solicitor

	Research sample %	Murch's sample %
Recommended by friend	21	28
Recommended by family	15	22
Already had a solicitor (e.g. for house purchase)	15	13
Via Citizens Advice Bureau	13	9 (incl. social workers)
Solicitor was a friend	7	–
Noticed a legal office	7	12
Telephone directory	7	4
Asked Legal Aid HQ	6	8
Other (social worker/ voluntary organisation)	4	–
Source forgotten/no information	5	4
	(n=113)	(n=102)

In this sample, 44 (73 per cent) of the 60 defenders had consulted a solicitor, in addition to all of the 60 pursuers. Before analysing respondents' experiences of legal services and defenders' reasons for seeing solicitors, it is useful to examine how these 104 respondents had chosen a solicitor. There are 113 reports of finding solicitors because seven respondents had consulted two different legal firms and one had consulted three. This does not take into account those who consulted more than one solicitor within one firm, either because of mobility of professional staff or because of different specialisms such as house purchase. The methods of choosing a solicitor may be compared with those used by the 102 petitioners (i.e. pursuers) in Murch's sample (Murch, 1977).

The seven who had consulted two solicitors were four men (two pursuers and two defenders) and three women (two pursuers and one defender). Some of these had visited one solicitor at about the time of marital separation and had later chosen a different one to start or to discuss divorce proceedings. Others had gone almost straight from one solicitor to another. Reasons for change within both groups had been that the first solicitor had died or that his advice was unpalatable (for instance, that property should be divided between the spouses). A young, childless wife-pursuer had seen three different solicitors. The first, a colleague of the solicitor who had purchased her house for her, told her she could either spend a lot of money and divorce her husband for adultery or wait for two years and divorce by consent. Two years later, she consulted a second solicitor (because 'I wasn't very keen on the other one'). She described him as not very helpful – 'when I mentioned Legal Aid, he wasn't very keen on it'. So she then saw a third solicitor, recommended by a friend who had been divorced, and she was satisfied with his explanation that it was not worthwhile applying for Legal Aid on her salary.

Thirty five (58 per cent) of the pursuers had had their expenses paid wholly or partially by Legal Aid. These were 11 (37 per cent) of the 30 husbands and 24 (80 per cent) of the 30 wives. Some of them had paid a big contribution towards the total cost: 'They charged me over £300 as it is. I can't see them (i.e. Legal Aid fund) paying much.' In one childless divorce which had been defended on its merits until shortly before proof, the wife-pursuer on Legal Aid had paid a substantial proportion of the total cost of nearly £700. Some pursuers had enquired about Legal Aid but had been told by solicitors that their income would make them ineligible. An application for Legal Aid could cause a three month delay in divorce proceedings.

An overwhelming majority were satisfied with their solicitors' services, many having had only one or two consultations and having been happy to leave their solicitors to do whatever was necessary to process the divorce. Pursuers (93 per cent) were rather more likely than defenders (82 per cent) to have found their solicitors helpful.

Murch (1977) reported that 92 per cent of his petitioner sample had been satisfied with their solicitors' services.

There was no difference between the numbers of husbands and of wives who were satisfied (88 per cent of each) nor between age groups at divorce.

There was, however, a significant difference between the social classes' satisfaction with legal services, those in classes IV and V being considerably less satisfied than others: 95 per cent of social classes I and II combined, 93 per cent of class III and 76 per cent of classes IV and V combined reported satisfaction.

Pursuers

Pursuers were generally uncritical of solicitors, 93 per cent having considered them helpful. Consultations had been about evidence of marital breakdown, about financial provision and about the children of the marriage.

Since the pursuers all achieved their divorces, it might have been assumed that they had all appreciated professional help. For most this was so. They saw their solicitors as doing all that was required in providing a professional service which did not need to be fully understood. 'I just spoke to a lawyer and he fixed it up. Then I never had anything to do with it until it was finished.' Such a situation was the easiest for both the pursuer and the solicitor and yet, because it was easy, it did not lead to much warmth of appreciation.

At least eleven pursuers visited a solicitor soon after marital separation (i.e. from two days to two months after) to start divorce proceedings; their spouses did not attempt to effect a reconciliation, nor to defend, apart from varying the financial proposals.

A further sixteen pursuers also consulted a solicitor soon after separation. Five of these were selling or buying houses. Twelve (including one of the house purchasers) had asked for legal advice about a divorce and had learned that they had no grounds and would have to wait for at least two years. This did not cause much concern. 'It is quite easy. You wait for two years and then get a divorce' or 'seemingly you have to wait for two years'. Most had later obtained their spouses' consent to divorce, but two had averred desertion.

While most had taken for granted whatever help their solicitors had given, some had been more actively appreciative: 'The first time I went, I never thought I had grounds for divorce. It was him that told me I'd get it for mental cruelty.' Three pursuers – only 5 per cent – had felt better or 'kind of eased' after talking to a solicitor: even though there was no immediate legal remedy for them, they had experienced a sense of relief at finding a sympathetic adviser. Solicitors were not expected to provide emotional support.

A few pursuers had been critical of their solicitors: 'At first, I felt he was a bit pushing. I suppose because I was upset on the first day and he kept firing questions at you and you can't remember everything.' 'I found him very difficult to talk to. He was always telling you what you should do and he told me I had no grounds because I had no witnesses.' Some pursuers did not inform solicitors of a change of address after starting divorce proceedings, and were aggrieved that they had not received legal communications.

Delay had usually been accepted philosophically: 'I knew them things take time.' However, two pursuers who had questioned the delay in obtaining their divorces had both been told that their files had been lost, in both cases apparently because of confusion over two with the same name. One of them, a young mother aged 22, had been taken aback to be visited by her doctor who said he had had a letter from her solicitor (so she understood) that she had been in hospital after a suicide attempt. 'My notes had got mixed up with someone else's.' Recalling this mistake, she treated it as a joke.

Four wife-pursuers had, after legal advice, changed the grounds on which they had intended to divorce their husbands. Three had changed from allegations of adultery to grounds of desertion, unreasonable behaviour and separation (with consent), respectively, while one waited two years for divorce by consent but was then advised by her solicitor to divorce for adultery with no risk of her husband refusing the necessary consent. In twelve other divorces, the defender had started

proceedings as a pursuer, but had dropped them. The net change in grounds for
those twelve was four divorces after two years separation and one after two years
desertion, instead of five for adultery.

One other potential wife-pursuer had asked for legal advice but:

> I disliked their whole attitude. I suppose they have to try
> to protect their clients. They tried to suggest I should
> sue for divorce on grounds of cruelty, but that was out of
> the question because of my husband's profession. The lawyer
> was trying to stir things up. In the end my husband
> arranged the divorce and I just signed my agreement ... It
> was a very unpleasant experience. The coldness of their
> attitude was rather depressing ... If I had allowed the
> lawyers to set up the divorce as they wanted, it would have
> damaged the relationship with my husband, they were so
> clinical.

While some thought divorce was too easy ('I can't help thinking, it is so painless
to get a divorce'), others thought it should be made even easier. A bus driver
said:

> This two years' separation is a lot of nonsense. If you
> can't make your marriage work, you ought to be able to end
> it without waiting two years. One year would be enough. No
> one would go back after a year apart.

However, two couples in the sample had come together after a year's separation,
finally separating after some further years. There have been suggestions in
England as well as in Scotland that divorce should be available solely on the
evidence of one year's separation.

Defenders

The main reason for defenders consulting solicitors was to dispute the financial
arrangements proposed in the Summons or to arrange for the amicable division of
property.

Six husbands and three wives had wanted legal information about divorce, or
clarification of the details in the Summonses they had received.

Twelve husbands and seven wives had had legal discussions about finance.

The four husbands and eight wives who had sought to initiate divorce proceedings,
had been overtaken by their spouses's actions for divorce or had not had the heart
to press accusations of adultery, or had been advised by solicitors that their
spouses had better evidence for divorce actions.

No defenders had disputed custody, and few had disagreed with proposed access to
children. Three wives had consulted solicitors about their children, two of them
to request access and one to resist her husband's request for access. All the
other defenders had accepted the proposed arrangements, including a negative
acceptance of no legal provision for access. Some trusted their ex-spouses to
allow access. Seven fathers and one mother were not interested in seeing their
children.

Finally, two husbands had hoped to defend charges of unreasonable behaviour, and one of them had continued to try to defend for nearly three years.

Sixteen defenders (27 per cent) had not consulted a solicitor. Seven of these were childless and had agreed the terms of divorce with their spouses. Nine had children. These nine were six men and three women, of whom one woman had a child living with her. None had wanted to consult a solicitor about financial provision or the care of their children who all (except for one two year old boy) were in touch with both parents.

Half of the 27 per cent of defenders who did not consult a solicitor about any aspect of their divorce, had consented to divorce after two years' separation and had seen no need for professional advice.

Two defenders had had informal discussion with legal friends. Others had shown a lack of interest towards the process of divorce. This apathy sometimes extended to the question of contact with their children.

One wife, who had not consulted a solicitor, said 'it costs too much money, which is why I allowed my husband to divorce me for desertion, because it would cost him, not me.' Others who had consulted a solicitor had also been deterred by fear of expense from returning for further legal advice. 'Perhaps a lot of people lose a lot of their rights that way,' or 'every time a lawyer writes a letter it costs money. I had a bill from the lawyer each time.'

The 44 defenders (73 per cent) who had consulted solicitors were almost equally divided between the spouses: 21 out of 30 husbands and 23 out of 30 wives.

Adultery was the most likely ground of marital breakdown to have taken a defender to a solicitor, although none had denied the adultery.

Defenders in social class III were the most likely to have consulted a solicitor; half of those who had not consulted a solicitor were in social classes IV and V, although only 30 per cent of all defenders were in those social classes. We have already seen that social classes IV and V had been significantly less satisfied than others with legal services. On this evidence, members of the working class seem more reluctant than others to seek legal advice about divorce and, if they do seek it, are less likely to be satisfied.

Whether or not there were children of the marriage made no difference to whether a defender consulted a solicitor: it has already been noted that nine with children had not done so.

Financial Provision

Any financial provision for children and spouses within this study was in favour of wives.

Only 40 per cent of wife-pursuers interviewed and 12 per cent of wife-defenders had children living with them. Less than half of these pursuers and only one of these defenders had anything to say about their solicitor's efforts to gain an award of aliment for their children. There seemed to be a general lack of concern by these mothers: some said that an award would make no difference to them because they were in receipt of social security and that the DHSS would therefore claim any aliment; others were already receiving regular payments from their husbands and saw no advantage in these being legalised; others doubted whether their husbands would pay, particularly when the husbands were thought to be unemployed.

Parents were not asked what aliment had been awarded by the court, but some offered information. Awards reported varied from £3 per week (father a dental technician) to £8 per week (fathers a 20 year old labourer and a 22 year old gas-fitter) for one child families, and from £4 per child per week (labourer father) to £8 per child per week (father a factory machine operator) for four child families. The general attitude of wives seemed to be that they were not interested in awards of aliment, and that they did not understand the long-term implications. One wife, who had received £5 a week from her husband for each of her two children during the year from separation to divorce, said that, unknown to her, her lawyer had asked for 'too much' (£8 per child) and her husband had then consulted a lawyer too. She said she believed the lawyers had sorted out what her husband should pay for the children, but that she was not consulted. Indeed, several defenders and pursuers appeared to have had little understanding of financial transactions between solicitors.

Several wives had rejected legal advice to ask their husbands for more than they had been paying voluntarily before divorce, although these sums had been eroded by inflation.

There had been a little more interest from husbands than from wives in periodical allowances (i.e. a regular payment by one spouse for the maintenance of the other). Wives, again, did not seem to appreciate the potential long-term addition to their income. Husbands who appeared willing to contribute to their children's upbringing were relieved when their solicitors persuaded their wives' solicitors to drop a request for an allowance for their wives, perhaps as part of a bargain for the husband's agreement to divorce.

One husband-defender had been maintaining his children but not his wife during the separation. Shortly before the divorce, so he said, he had a phone call from his solicitor asking "do you want me to pay your wife?" 'I said no, but he said it was usually the procedure and could I make it a fiver, so I said yes.' His wife also reported this last minute change of heart, saying that her husband's solicitor had come to court to confirm the offer to her solicitor. This weekly allowance of £5 to the wife appeared to have been treated lightly by all concerned, and was typical of attitudes to financial provision.

Couples who had owned the matrimonial home had usually arranged, before separation, how they would divide the proceeds of a house sale, or how one retaining possession would compensate the other. They had then asked solicitors to make the necessary arrangements. Legal advice to one wife-defender was that she was 'entitled to one third under the law' of the value of the matrimonial home. She kept quiet about this advice, having already agreed with her husband to split the value equally between them.

Two husbands described incidents which suggested that they may have had question-able advice from a solicitor. One, a defender, had mentioned the divorce Summons when consulting a solicitor about something different and had understood that the judge would award him half of the contents of the house in which his wife still lived. The other, a pursuer, had consulted 'a chap I was at school with, to find out how I'd stand when a divorce came through ... He told me she'd get half of everything, including the house.' Incredulous, because 'she was the one at fault', he moved on to another legal firm. Where a wife has no legal financial rights, the court usually awards her about one third of the total assets and one third of the difference between the two incomes, but there is no hard and fast rule. These cases suggest that there is a possibility of receiving inaccurate advice from a solicitor who does not normally deal with divorce.

Expenses were normally awarded against the husband if he were employed. Some couples had come to an agreement in advance that they would share the expenses, either equally or in the proportion of two thirds by the husband and one third by the wife. In those cases, the pursuer's solicitor was informed of the arrangement.

One husband-defender reported that he and his wife had come to an agreement through their solicitors that he would not be asked to pay any of the expenses. 'She was divorcing me because she wanted rid of me so she could stay with the other bloke.' His wife had had Legal Aid and it seemed possible that he was under a misapprehension about liability for expenses. Several husbands had thought that divorce was expensive. 'You pay £3 to get there and £300 to get out again; £3 to say I do and £300 to say I won't.' Some complained about the difference in cost between a divorce in Scotland and one in England.

Experience at Court

Three quarters of pursuers interviewed went to court for their divorce hearings before the system was changed in May 1978 to evidence being taken by affidavit. Attendance at court had no direct relevance to this study, but it was a significant event. For some, it resulted in a release of emotional tension and, although a stressful occasion, it was indirectly a source of help. 'It was a sad day, although there was no love in my heart for my ex-husband. The relief afterwards - I can't describe how I felt. The numbness and tension just goes.' It is worth recording the experiences of some of these pursuers as a part of the social history of divorce, now that very few actions reach the court.

For many of the 47 pursuers who attended court, the day of divorce was traumatic, an experience denied to defenders. For some, there had been a matrimonial offence and for others there had been similar incidents as evidence of marital breakdown. When a divorce was based on adultery or on cruelty (later replaced by 'unreasonable behaviour') it was the 'innocent' rather than the 'guilty' party who was questioned and who had briefly to re-live the pain and hurt. 'It was for cruelty, and the worst part was going to court and having to drag it all out again'.

Some pursuers had assumed that they would see a familiar face at court; others had been told that an agent would deputise. Most had been nervous, in an unfamiliar setting, and did not understand the procedure until it was explained on the spot. Some agents did not locate their clients for quite a time, while the tension mounted. There were difficulties for an agent who had several divorces in different courts on the same morning, but pursuers did not appreciate this, and could feel alarmed. A lorry driver phoned his solicitor after waiting for an hour and 20 minutes 'because there was nae sign of him and other people's lawyers were coming in and having a blether'. A wife had been told:

> an agent would come and talk to me beforehand, but no agent
> came. I heard my name being called and no one was there. I
> was petrified. Then a man in a wig came along with a woman
> carrying a brief-case. These two wanted to hold up the case
> for a few minutes, but the man at the door said "hurry up,
> he's in a bad temper".

The crowded conditions in the waiting areas had upset several pursuers. One wife and her witness had had to take turns in sitting down for an hour. A clerical worker said 'my mother and I sat in the corridor, which was jam-packed with people. There were lawyers walking in and out and names being called out over the Tannoy. There was no place to speak in private to your lawyer.'

Television programmes, experiences of other courts, and misguided friends had been

responsible for false expectations of the court. A 22 year old wife had 'imagined
it would be like courts on TV, with a big jury.' Indeed, she had assumed that her
case would last all morning because she had been told that she would probably be
out by lunchtime. Others had expected a more informal setting: 'I had been prepared to talk to someone across a table, not to stand in a witness box and talk up
to a judge.' 'I thought you'd go into a wee room with a desk. I didn't expect a
court.'

Nervousness was understandable, but some comments demonstrate the fear and even
guilt felt by pursuers:

> It was a terrifying experience. I've never been so nervous
> in all my life. I'll never forget it. I felt like a
> criminal standing up in the witness box. My mind just went,
> I was so shaky. I'd never been in a police station, let
> alone a court room. I don't think I'll ever get married
> again in case it ever came to divorce again.

And:

> It was the most degrading and horrible experience I've ever
> had. I hated my husband that day for making me go through
> that.

Uncertainty over their children's future caused some concern:

> I was quite worried because custody was not mentioned. I
> expected the judge to sum up. When you sit in a dentist's
> chair, they tell you when you're finished.

Many complained of not hearing what was said in court and of not knowing whether
or not their divorce had been granted or on what terms until they met their
solicitor again afterwards. One wife told me that 'maintenance' had not been
mentioned, but she later found on her divorce certificate that her husband was to
pay her £8 per child per week although he would be in prison for at least another
two years.

To many of these pursuers, divorce proceedings in court were an undignified and
painful way of ending a marriage.

Although an advocate (counsel) was employed for every divorce, only three quarters
of the pursuers in the sample had had their divorce actions heard in open court
and had had any opportunity to meet their counsel. For the remaining one quarter,
the summons had been drafted by counsel on the evidence taken by the solicitor on
affidavit and the pursuer had not attended court. A judge could have requested a
hearing in court, but this had not happened. Therefore, any possible experience of
meeting counsel was limited to 47 (78 per cent) pursuers.

In theory, these 47 pursuers should have had an opportunity of meeting the counsel
who would question them in court. In fact, 13 (28 per cent) said that they had not
had any such opportunity. A further 17 (36 per cent) had met their counsel, often
only exchanging names as they were led into court. The remaining 17 (36 per cent)
did not mention their counsel, but it seems likely that up to half of the pursuers
did not speak to, nor meet, their counsel until they came face to face in court.

Pursuers were not always clear about the function of their counsel. A known
solicitor might be present 'but it was another man who asked the questions.' 'My
lawyer was there, but he appointed a barrister to speak for him.' Occasionally,

pursuers had been conscious that there had been a last minute change of counsel, because their own was held up in another court when their case was called.

Contact with counsel was minimal and transitory, and only one pursuer had expressed any appreciation: 'My lady counsel was the nicest person I met all day. A very warm person.' A husband who had not met his counsel beforehand had nevertheless found it 'comforting to see someone fighting on my behalf.'

Legally, there was no necessity for counsel to meet the pursuer before asking questions based on the information which the pursuer had provided. In practice, pursuers would have felt a little more at ease if they had had an opportunity at least to be introduced to their counsel before going into court. 'I didn't know anyone in court. They were all strangers. I think I'd have been a bit more relaxed if I'd seen the counsel before. I was so nervous, I had to hold on to the box.'

Misunderstandings

By the time of interview, all respondents should have received an extract of their divorce decree. All had earlier had a copy of the summons. Yet some did not know whether there was any provision for access (possibly it had not been requested and there was none). Some did not know the grounds of divorce (one husband-pursuer said he had no idea, but supposed it must have been for adultery: his wife said it was for cruelty). Several wives on Legal Aid did not know that expenses had been awarded against their husbands: 'They never said anything about costs, but I don't want to know, as long as it's not coming out of my pocket.' Some husbands were falsely confident that, as defenders, they would have nothing to pay: a rude shock could have awaited them. A few respondents produced their extract decree to show to me, and together we discovered that some of this missing information was already in their possession but not understood.

Pursuers were sometimes unaware that defenders may not know for a further 21 days that they are divorced, nor what financial provisions or access arrangements have been made. They tended to assume that any legal changes in weekly aliment or in hours of access would take effect immediately, whereas the defenders may not know about such changes until three weeks after the divorce has been granted. Some defenders were upset to discover that, for three weeks, they had been divorced while they thought they were still married. This may seem a small point, but it appeared to cause some distress to defenders.

Two wife-defenders said they did not know that they had been divorced. Both knew that a divorce action was pending. One had had 'a letter saying she would have to appear in court' which may have been her interpretation of 'cause appearance to be entered on your behalf.' She was amazed and delighted to learn from me that she had been divorced for seven weeks. Probably the postman had been less assiduous than I had, in tracing these two wives to new addresses.

Conclusions

Many respondents seemed not to have understood what their solicitors had told them and, indeed, not to have been concerned about this. They tended to hand over particulars of their marriage, and to be content to wait until the legal machine churned out a divorce. They were more concerned with changing their status from being married to being divorced, than with trying to understand the long-term legal or financial implications. It might have been appreciated if they had had a simple written explanation, before the divorce hearing, of any custody, access and financial provisions proposed in the divorce summons.

The opening paragraph of a summons is almost incomprehensible to a layman, whose vocabulary may not include words such as 'pursuer', 'crave' and 'decree'. The word 'divorce' is not mentioned. Other phrases led to misunderstanding: 'cause appearance to be entered on your behalf' did not refer to the physical appearance of the defender nor of his representative. If it is necessary to retain such archaic language, it seems essential that a translation into plain, everyday English should be provided. The lawyers understand the procedure, and the summons is not produced for their benefit but for that of their clients.

It should be made crystal clear to husbands, and in advance, that they are likely to be liable for the considerable expenses of a divorce action, even when they are defenders. If a wife-pursuer is granted Legal Aid, her husband will almost certainly have to repay the cost of the divorce action to the Legal Aid fund. This, too, should surely be explained with care, and at an early stage. Most divorce defenders have no previous experience from which to understand these financial obligations. It should not be necessary for them either to be left in ignorance until after the divorce is granted, or to have to consult a solicitor about such basic matters.

Solicitors who have become familiar with divorce procedure might be surprised that one middle-aged wife-defender described an interview with a solicitor as her 'first brush with the law'. For divorce solicitors and their agents, some training in understanding human behaviour might help them to recognise more easily and to alleviate their clients' distress and fears. It should not be difficult for the court to devise a solution to the misunderstandings caused by the three week delay in informing defenders of their divorce (a delay intended, in theory, to allow defenders the opportunity to appeal against the decree with fresh evidence). Finally, it would also be useful to provide a very simple leaflet about court proceedings, preferably illustrated, for those few who still have to attend a divorce court.

DOCTORS

Half of the sample (59) had something to say about their experiences of their doctors (i.e. general practitioners) as sources of help in difficulties consequent on marital breakdown. They were 17 husbands (28 per cent) and 42 wives (70 per cent), or 32 pursuers (53 per cent) and 27 defenders (45 per cent).

The difference between husbands and wives in consulting their doctors was statistically significant. Murch found that 56 per cent of his men and women petitioners (i.e. pursuers) had consulted their doctors (Murch, 1975). Chester interviewed women petitioners, of whom 64 per cent had sought medical help (Chester, 1973), compared with 73 per cent of wife-pursuers in the present study.

Husbands were more likely to have consulted their doctors if their wives had left them than if they had left home themselves. The opposite was so for wives, who were more likely to have consulted doctors if they had left home than if their husbands had left them. Five husbands and four wives (including both halves of three couples) had left home at the same time as their spouses: of them, two wives and no husbands had consulted doctors.

Slightly over half of those who had custody of their children had consulted their general practitioners (five out of ten husbands and 21 out of 31 wives). Those married for less than four years and those aged up to 25 at divorce were the least likely to have consulted doctors. Social classes I and II were the most likely to have seen their doctors.

General practitioners had been found helpful by 34 per cent of the sample (10 husbands and 31 wives) and unhelpful by 15 per cent (7 husbands and 11 wives). Most writers do not give comparable figures, but 15 per cent of Blaxter's respondents (all of whom, being disabled, had had contact with general practitioners) had appeared to be dissatisfied with their doctors and 40 per cent to 'have had exceptionally good relationships' (Blaxter, 1976).

Appreciation of medical care had steadily decreased with social class (from 75 per cent of class I to 25 per cent of class V). Respondents who were aged over 25 at divorce or whose de facto marriages had lasted for more than four years were not only more likely to have consulted their doctors, but also more likely than others to have found them helpful.

Reasons for Consulting General Practitioners

Only five husbands and three wives had gone to their doctors in order to talk specifically about their marriage difficulties. One man said he had gone 'to discuss basic difficulties with the marriage. They say you should go to your doctor or minister.' Another man 'ended having to talk to someone' so he had gone to his doctor, having rejected the idea of talking to his parents or his sister.

Overwhelmingly the most common reason for seeing doctors was 'nerves'. It was not always possible to discern why a respondent had sought medical aid or advice, but eight husbands and 19 wives said they had consulted their doctors about 'nerves' or feelings of depression. 'I had to go to him when I found I was living off my nerves,' 'I was bad with my nerves' or 'my nerves were pretty shattered.'

In addition, two husbands and six wives had seen their doctors because they were having difficulty in sleeping. 'I just wanted to sleep. I spent most nights in the kitchen drinking tea,' 'it was affecting my health; I couldn't sleep at nights' or 'I was feeling edgy and not sleeping at nights.'

After separation, seven men and three women in the sample had all begun to drink more than they had previously done. It seems probable that even more had done so, since this was information fortuitously offered. Some claimed to have dealt with the problem on their own, without any outside help. Others had contacted Alcoholics Anonymous (one), Samaritans (one) or their doctor (three).

One man had had no hesitation in presenting his problem to a woman doctor whom he saw about five times. While he had been able to sit and talk to her, he had looked on 'a load of tablets' as the more relevant treatment which 'helped in a way' but he considered that he had stopped drinking mainly by his own efforts. A nurse had presented with 'tiredness and depression' until her doctor asked whether she had any problems. Then she had been able to talk about her drinking and had found him helpful.

Of the ten men who had custody of their children, one admitted that he had started drinking heavily after his wife had left him. He used to buy bottles of wine and would be flat out when his children came home from school. When a kindly neighbour spoke to him about it and told him to 'get a hold of yourself' something clicked and he immediately was able to stop drinking, he said. He had drunk because he was depressed – not only had his wife left the family, but he had not been able to take up new employment because he had to look after his children. Consulting his doctor about something else later on, he found himself explaining what had happened earlier and he told me 'I should have went to the doctor. I never bothered to go near him. The doctor said I should have come to him with the drinking. I never knew he could have helped.'

Meanwhile, his wife had also admitted to drinking heavily because she was lonely.
She had given up her job as well as her family and was living in a bed-sitter
with her new partner.

> I started drinking. I was really hitting the bottle hard. I
> had nothing to do when P. was on three shifts, so I began to
> take two or three Carlsbergs and half a bottle of rum to my
> room. I couldn't stop. Then I'd have five or six Mickey
> Finns.

She went to the pub, always the same one, as soon as it opened, morning and
evening. Then, thinking she might lose her boyfriend because of her drinking, she
managed sometimes to walk past the pub and to delay going in. She succeeded in
breaking her habit when she began visiting a married sister. 'Her kids were a real
help. I'd go to anyone with kids. I started buying myself cuddly toys. I used to
sit and nurse them.' She did not consult her doctor about her drinking, but did
see him regularly for 'nerves' for which she had a steady supply of tranquillisers.

Two men had had easy access to drink at their work and had taken advantage of this.
One had worked for nine years as a whisky chiller and described his drinking as
'an easy way out' after his wife had left him. He rejected his doctor's advice to
'pack in' the drink and he refused his employer's offer to transfer him to another
department in the same firm, since he knew that he would still find his drink. The
other man who drank at work was a hospital cook. 'After I had to give the house up,
I had nowhere to go and I started hitting the drink. I was drinking every night
till 3 o'clock in the morning.'

A man whose marriage had lasted for three months had had 'the odd Scotch. I did
drink too much for a while. I lost weight, about one and a half stone. I didn't
eat and I drank too much for about three months.' He looked astonished by the
suggestion that he might have sought help in cutting down his drinking. Another
man 'drank a little more ... It was difficult coming home to an empty house and
starting cooking.' He stopped his habit of having a couple of pints on the way
home by getting an evening job in a bar.

The youngest self-admitted drinker was a girl who, having left her husband when
she was 20, 'went to the drink a wee while. I was getting quite a heavy drinker ...
I stopped it because I had to pay my rent and gas and light.'

Most of these drinkers had not looked for medical help.

Other respondents had complained to their doctors about loss of weight, or
indigestion. Only one had consulted a doctor about the welfare of children, in
asking for advice about whether one of her four children should live with her
husband.

Treatment

Almost without exception, those who had consulted their general practitioners
appeared to have been prescribed tranquillisers (eight named valium and two
librium), sleeping pills, 'pills' or 'tablets'. Two had also had 'waking up pills'.
Some had decided in advance what kind of treatment they needed. 'I went for a
nerve tonic' or 'I had to go in a mental sense, to explain why I needed certain
medication.' Many had been satisfied and had expected nothing more. Three claimed
not to have used whatever was prescribed: 'I knew what it was for, so of course I
didn't take it.' One husband said 'It's quite handy for a doctor to give you
tablets or to give you two months off work even when you don't need it.'

Similar evidence was reported by Parkes (1972) that doctors were expected to treat widows' psychological symptoms of grief with sedatives or tranquillisers, and that this was all that doctors had usually done; by Chester (1973) that the most common treatment for wives whose marriages had broken down was 'with psychotropic or hypnotic drugs'; and by Ferri and Robinson (1976).

A few had had many repeat prescriptions and, while using them, had felt some unease. 'I was worried about him dishing out 200 valium at a time' or 'he was a bit too willing to carry on prescribing. I thought I could get repeat prescriptions too easily. I cut them down myself in the end. I didn't like the side effects. They worked by clipping off one's emotions at the top and the bottom.' Although some had had relatives who took charge of their tablets, three had taken overdoses because of the marital breakdown. One, a wife of 28, had possibly not intended harming herself, since her new partner had been present and he had dosed her with salted water; her doctor had then refused to prescribe any further drugs. A husband of 29, however, had taken twenty phenobarbitone only two days after calling in the police because he was afraid of harming himself. A neighbour who had his key had found him. After release from hospital, he had had no contact with his general practitioner.

While respondents had been reluctant to discuss marriage difficulties with their doctors ('I used to say I don't really know what's bothering me'), most had not considered that there was any need to explain what lay behind their 'nerves'. Many of the doctors seemed also to have accepted symptoms at their face value without any further questioning.

Two husbands and ten wives had found their doctors emotionally, as well as professionally, supportive. In some cases, these had been family doctors of long standing, well known to respondents as 'the sort of doctor you can talk to'. For some, it was a relief to be asked for more information and to be able to talk about their marriages. A middle-aged wife said 'I was going to be so calm. I'd been going to him for a sore throat, and when he asked if my throat was bad again, I burst into tears. He said "take your time" ...' She saw her doctor, whom she described as a friend, on two or three further occasions.

'He was a great doctor for listening. He was fantastic. He'd a big pile of patients waiting,' said an ex-barmaid who had been relieved that her doctor had never suggested she should return to her husband and children. For her, as for many others, support was appreciated because the doctor did not question her actions and therefore gave the implicit approval which she required. Support was none the less valuable, since it gave the confidence to continue with the marital separation. The opportunity to let off steam was also appreciated: 'You could rant and rave if you wanted,' said a young secretary of visits to the two doctors in her practice, one of whom had suggested getting help from a marriage counsellor.

Practical advice was acceptable only if it was what the patient wanted to hear. Three wives were relieved that their doctors had, apparently, advised them to leave their husbands. A fourth had already done so and disagreed strongly with her family doctor who suggested that she might return to her husband for the sake of her baby daughter, whom she had taken with her. She also disapproved of the sleeping pills which he prescribed, since she did not want to risk not hearing her baby if she woke in the night. 'I didn't think my doctor believed in things like that.' She had just wanted someone to talk to, she said, and had felt let down.

Several couples had different doctors from each other, having made no change on marriage. One of these wives had thought it important to talk to a doctor who knew her husband.

> My husband's doctor has been the best. He's a real family
> doctor. He took time to talk and he even tried to speak to
> my husband. My own doctor would have been just as good, but
> he didn't know my husband so it would have been a waste of
> time.

Others had been asked why, for instance, they could not sleep, but their doctors
did not then discuss further the broken marriages. It may be that these respondents
were unwilling to be drawn. A woman said 'My GP gave me anything I wanted, librium,
mogadon, but he doesn't encourage you to talk. I have a highly developed facade
mechanism,' and she thought her doctor had never known how upset she was. And a
man reported:

> Three months after the separation, I was very depressed
> about it all and was on pills for a while. I would have said
> my doctor was helpful within the limitations of time ...
> From the point of view that I got the appropriate pills, the
> doctor was helpful, but not terribly much more than that.
> It's probably fair to say that was all I needed. I was going
> through phases when I burst into tears.

Some behaviour, such as crying, was seen as inappropriate. A woman clerical officer
had deliberately not explained the reasons for her sleeping difficulties: 'I didn't
feel like talking. I would have got emotional and didn't want to do that in a
doctor's surgery.'

Seven doctors had suggested that others might be better able to help than they
were. One had successfully referred a patient to a partner 'because he didn't have
time to cope'. Two wives whose doctors had suggested that they might see a
marriage counsellor had not done so - one believing that such help should not be
necessary and the other passing on the idea to her husband, rather than acting on
it herself.

Both halves of one couple and two other wives were the only respondents who
volunteered that they had been referred to a psychiatrist because of marital
difficulties. The couple saw different psychiatrists at different times and
neither was involved in treatment for the other. The husband had found that 'it is
very true that if you talk to anyone about a problem you can solve it'. His wife
had seen a psychiatrist five or six times as an outpatient after taking an overdose, but had not found this helpful. 'I didn't think I needed help. I didn't feel
I had anything to tell him, but I told my husband I would go.' On the other hand,
she did think it unfair to burden a general practitioner and 'if you want to talk,
it's better to see the right kind of doctor'. Of the other two wives, one had seen
a psychiatrist when she was arranging for the baby of the marriage to be adopted;
the other had suffered a severe depression. 'I'd went to see a psychiatrist. I
didn't fancy it at all. Even at that visit, I couldn't talk to the psychiatrist. I
just needed to talk and I wouldn't have been able to talk to her.' Three of these
four psychiatric patients had admitted the need to talk to someone, but only two
had found a psychiatrist helpful.

Another couple had both been in psychoanalysis during the marriage and both had
leaned on their analysts when the marriage was in difficulties. Both had found less
need for this intensive support after the final separation but had found it
important during a series of separations and reconciliations. The husband described
this support as double-edged, since the analysis hastened the inevitable breakdown
of the marriage.

Unhelpful General Practitioners

Some who gave their perceptions of their doctors had not consciously discussed marital problems with them but said, in effect, that this was nothing to do with their doctor, to whom they would take physical symptoms only.

Seven husbands (12 per cent) and eleven wives (18 per cent) had found their doctors unhelpful: of these, three husbands and five wives considered that their doctors had positively failed them. One young wife did not feel any lack of professional care but simply found her foreign doctor difficult to understand, which killed any discussion. Four respondents had felt let down when their doctors had not been willing to discuss the marriage: 'He didn't have much time and showed a degree of disinterest,' 'the doctor is not interested in your marriage, only in your health' or 'he's not much good; he's the type that's got the prescription written out before you've told him what's wrong with you.' Two wives had found their doctors even more positively unhelpful. One said, 'He gave me some tablets and told me it wouldn't help me, but he'd give me them anyway.' The other had gone to her doctor with a threatened miscarriage after a brief reconciliation during the period of separation. She was greatly taken aback when her doctor had asked who the father was. After losing the baby for which she had longed (and losing her husband too), she learned that her husband had earlier taken his girlfriend to the same doctor, who had assumed that the husband was still living with his girlfriend and had not returned to his wife.

General Practitioners not Consulted

Most of the 61 who had not considered consulting their doctors looked surprised by the suggestion that they might have done so. A few gave reasons, such as that the doctor was too busy ('he's all right to talk to, but let's face it, they've got an awful lot of patients'), that they were unqualified to help with marriage diffi-culties because of lack of personal experience ('doctors cannot help in the way you need. You need someone else who has experienced marital separation'), that they were too old ('my family doctor is in his sixties. I couldn't have turned to him at all') or that they already had access to medication (a labourer had helped himself first to his wife's valium and later to his mother's).

One husband and one wife voiced the belief that doctors no longer filled a traditional pastoral role. 'Doctors are not leaning posts like they used to be: they process you like lawyers. You are a health card, not a person.' Neither of them had any siblings, nor had either talked to their one available parent: one had leaned mainly on a colleague and the other on a cousin.

One third of the husbands and of the wives who did not consult their doctors had had emotional support from their mothers. Nearly half of those who did not consult doctors had had emotional support from friends, neighbours or colleagues, some-times as well as from mothers.

Additional Support

Of the 41 who had found general practitioners helpful, 12 had had emotional support from their mothers and from friends, neighbours or colleagues; 11 from mothers but not from friends, neighbours or colleagues; and 14 from friends, neighbours or colleagues but not from their mothers. Therefore in 37 out of 41 cases, general practitioners were overlapping one or more of the main informal sources of support. Twelve of the 30 who claimed to have had informal emotional support from only one source had also consulted their doctors about problems concerned with their marriages, seven of them finding their doctors to be helpful.

Conclusions

It was generally seen as acceptable to consult a doctor about a physical symptom
but not about an emotional one. In particular, 'nerves' were presented as physical,
often without any expectation of examining underlying emotional disturbances.
General practitioners were seen mainly as providers of instant practical help (in
the form of tranquillisers) or advice. Few respondents had expected their doctors
to be willing to discuss marriage difficulties or to have time to listen. There
was some evidence to suggest that there are general practitioners who do not
investigate the cause of 'nerves' or of sleeplessness, or who prefer not to pro-
long an appointment by allowing the patient to embark on a complicated story.

Doctors themselves provided evidence of this tendency in Byrne and Long's study
(1976). In 2500 tape-recorded consultations with general practitioners, the
authors showed that some doctors 'try hard to stop the flow' (p.60) and that
emotional problems provide difficulties for some doctors, whose training 'makes it
unlikely that he will be able to cope easily with a non-organic problem' (p.140).

Doctors who prefer not to involve themselves in lengthy consultations about
marital difficulties might consider referrals to someone else in the practice (a
partner, a health visitor or a social worker) or to another agency such as
marriage guidance. A positive offer to make an alternative appointment, especially
on the same premises, might lead to it being kept, and possibly to fewer return
visits for repeat prescriptions.

            CLERGY

Only 27 (22.5 per cent) of the total of 120 divorced respondents claimed any
church connections, and almost all of these were no longer active.

Respondents were not asked whether they belonged to any church, nor what their
religion was. They were asked whether they had had any help from a minister. Most
claimed not to have, or not to know, any minister. Those who had had any connection
with a church, however tenuous, usually explained why they had or had not sought
support there. Sixteen volunteered the information that they were, or had been,
Catholic including both spouses in four couples. Only three of these Catholics
(all husbands, one pursuer and two defenders) had a current connection with their
church. Eight others indicated a connection (three currently) with the Church of
Scotland, and three wives were respectively Episcopalian, Jewish and Mormon, all
actively.

Seven described emotional support from their church: one Catholic, four Church of
Scotland, one Jewish and one Mormon (two husbands and five wives). The Catholic
and the Mormon had both been converts to their respective churches after their
marriages had broken down.

Most of the professed Catholics no longer knew a priest and did not consider them
as a potential source of help with marital difficulties. 'I tend to think priests
wouldn't really understand, they're not experienced enough, they're just spiritual
and think marriage should go on regardless.' Two said they were denied the
sacraments because they were divorced. For one of these two, that was not
important (indeed, this was his third divorce) although he still attended his
church fortnightly. For the other, this rejection by his church seemed to weigh
more heavily than the rejection by his wife. The Catholic convert had been taken
to church by a girlfriend with whom he later lost touch. He had joined her church
and had been greatly supported by a weekly chat with a priest.

Two Church of Scotland wives were particularly appreciative of support from their ministers. One, a Sunday school teacher, had found it helpful to talk things over, although slightly inhibited by advice from her lawyer not to let her minister decide what action she should take. The other had not sought out her minister but had been visited by him: 'We just sort of talked. It was the fact that somebody cared.' The Mormon and Jewish wives, too, had been conscious that their churches cared and had been supported by this knowledge.

Some others reported that a minister or a priest had called once, on hearing of a marriage breakdown, but had not returned when their offers of support or of material help were not accepted.

Two wives had positively rejected offers of help from ministers. One had not replied to a letter from the man who had officiated at her wedding. The other had been another Sunday school teacher and was conscious that, in some way, she blamed her marriage breakdown on the minister who had married her. He had recently replaced the minister she had known and liked.

> I didn't want to speak to him. I said if there is a God, why did he do this to me? He came twice. He treated me as though it was a duty. I made it quite clear to him I didn't want to see him. I feel ashamed now when I think about it ... Since the split, I've never been back to church and I never will.

In one marriage, there had been alienation from both sets of parents because of religious differences which led to husband and wife breaking off attendance at the Church of Scotland and the Catholic church respectively.

Two respondents were visibly surprised to be asked whether they had had any help from the church and thought it a good idea: 'It never crossed my mind ... I've heard the minister is very nice to speak to.'

Conclusions

Those with church connections tended not to use them for support in failing marriages. Offers of help had been ignored or misunderstood by some respondents and not repeated by ministers or priests. Some of these respondents had been conscious of the need to talk to someone, but had not visualised their ministers in a pastoral role.

SOCIAL WORKERS

Social workers were not generally perceived as being available for help with marital problems, although 24 (20 per cent) reported contact with social workers (eight husbands and sixteen wives, including three couples). All had children under 16 and they were evenly distributed over the age range at divorce, but they came predominantly from the lower end of the social class range, 37 per cent of respondents in classes IV and V having had social workers, compared with 28 per cent of class III and 6 per cent of classes I and II.

These 24 respondents had seen social workers in connection with the following difficulties:

(a) Marital : 2 husbands, 2 wives
(b) Child care : 3 husbands, 11 wives
(c) Housing, furniture, finance, prison location : 3 husbands,
    4 wives

    TOTAL : 24 (one wife being recorded twice, in (a) and (b)).
Some had had only minimal contact, and eleven had not themselves asked for social
work services.

Looking first at the 13 respondents who had asked for social work help when their
marriages were in difficulties, most of them had made purely practical requests.
Three had presented specifically with marriage problems, five with problems about
children, three with requests for housing, one with money difficulties and one man
had unsuccessfully asked a prison social worker to prevent his removal to a prison
further from his wife.

Only two wives and one husband had taken the positive step of approaching a social
worker in order to talk about their marriages. Of these, only one, a wife, had
been appreciative of support given in response to her request for someone to call
'to try to sort things out'. '(the social worker) gave us plenty of time and was
trying to help ... I suppose her aim was to get us together. It seemed to me that
was what she was doing.' But when that social worker left the area, the wife
'didn't feel like going through it all again'. The one husband and the other wife
had both been disappointed. The man, with eventual custody of two teenage daughters,
had been concerned about the effect on the family of his wife's heavy drinking: 'I
went along to a social worker, but I don't think they interfere with marriages and
that ... I thought maybe a wee talk ...' The woman had seen a young social worker:
'She looked about 20. It was a waste of time. She could only say "think of the good
times, and try to patch up the marriage and think of the children".'

The five who had presented problems concerning children were two husbands and three
wives. One husband had taken the precaution of informing the social work department
that he had left his children with his mentally ill wife. Later, with a social
worker's support and with her practical help over housing, he gained custody of his
two children. Two wives and the second husband had wanted day care for small
children: two were found places but one wife was angry that she was offered only a
list of child-minders and that no social worker had visited her. She had cried for
help with a specific problem 'but no one bothered' although, to do the social work
department justice, she appeared to have had other resources available. The third
wife had had intermittent social work care for her daughter for seven years, and
therefore looked for further support after the marriage had broken down. She was
ambivalent in her feelings for her daughter: 'They were going to put her in a
Home ... I wanted her to go away but deep down I would miss her. I was miserable
and she was happy, and I thought why should I make myself miserable and depressed
because of her?' The most recent social worker had been rejected for suggesting an
application for local authority housing, so that mother and daughter did not have
to live on top of one another in a rented room and kitchen, where the mother
wanted to remain.

Three wives and one husband with housing or financial problems had applied to their
local social work offices. Two of the wives had been angered when offered a list
of guest houses or a house in an undesirable locality. A husband with a teenage son
had been grateful for practical help with housing and then with furnishing, but
said he had not discussed his marriage. The third wife was adamant that several
very helpful sessions with a social worker had been solely concerned with social
security. Encouraged by this support, she later 'put in for a social worker to
come to the house (about a truanting son) but they said they didn't do home visits
and I knew full well they did'.

Social Work Provided Unasked

Eleven respondents (three husbands and eight wives) were in touch with social
workers without having made a conscious decision to approach them. Mostly they had
had children referred to social workers. Only one seemed to have discussed the
marriage.

A husband aged 20 described how his wife (whom I failed to trace) 'wanted a social
worker to help us with our problems. She comes from a broken-up family, so she
knew social workers ... She told (the social worker) about what I was doing ...
She tried to get me cured instead of herself. I didn't think I needed a social
worker.' This attitude of dissociation from any responsibility for marital breakdown was shared by several others who had seen marriage guidance counsellors.

Two husbands and eight wives had, unasked, had social workers assigned to their
children for problems apparently arising from the marital breakdown. Two of these
wives had had social work support for unusual problems. One had successfully
applied for her baby (born shortly before the marriage, which had then lasted for
only six weeks) to be adopted. Without the baby, there would probably have been no
marriage, and the husband had reported no children of the marriage. The other had
a severely handicapped child, and had been so appreciative of her social worker's
support that she thought single parents without a handicapped child would be at a
greater disadvantage than she had been.

I interviewed two couples whose children had been under social work supervision
because their mothers had neglected them. There was some similarity between these
families: in both cases, the fathers had left a baby and a toddler with their
wives and had returned to their own parents. Both mothers had been visited by
social workers because of reported neglect of children, and foster parents had
been found for the children of both families. Both mothers volunteered the information, early in their interviews, that they'd been visited by a social worker,
but neither sounded enthusiastic about any professional support. One went so far
as to say that her social worker could have been a great help 'but we got a bit
involved ... he was so young and attractive. He was always in a hurry; he never
came when he said he would.' At that time, she had been aged 18, and a mother of
two, and had looked on the social worker as a potential boyfriend.

Both fathers had eventually gained custody of their children, who had been the
subject of Children's Hearings. One of the fathers had had a succession of social
workers and he gave the impression that he had humoured them without being
particularly appreciative ('One woman came a couple of times but she was bloody
hopeless. She didna ken what to ask you. She just sat there'). The other father
had had only one social worker who 'never did much. I asked if he could get the
children into a nursery ... but he never got in contact with me.'

Two mothers had had social work support for children with behaviour problems at
school, but one had looked on the social work appointments as a corrective for
her eight year old son, while the other had been most grateful for help with a
teenage daughter who had been taunted because her father was in prison. 'The
school and social work department are closely linked up, so now I have a social
worker on my back but he's very nice and solely concerned with A. who is not
responsible for what she does or says.'

Most of these parents sounded rather remote from their social workers and perhaps
saw them only as necessary visitors with whom they were forced to co-operate.

Mention should be made of one husband with custody of four children. He acquired
two social workers, both unintentionally. He went to what he thought was the CAB

but discovered it was 'the welfare'. There, a male social worker put him in touch with a lawyer, and negotiated with DHSS for him, and also helped him when he was in financial difficulties. But that social worker never visited the home and never met the children. By chance, one day another social worker came to the house in a search for a different family. She subsequently befriended this man's four children and took them for an outing once every month at weekends. He was more than grateful for this girl's care.

In all, social work support had been appreciated, to some extent, by 15 respondents (five husbands and ten wives), including nine who had not requested social work services.

Conclusions

There seemed to be little demand for support from the statutory social services in what were seen to be specifically marital difficulties. The position might well be different in England and Wales, where matrimonial conciliation has long been a mandatory responsibility of Probation Officers (Jarvis, 1974), and where welfare officers have been attached to Divorce Courts since 1957. Neither of these functions have ever been established in Scotland, where the probation service was merged with social work services in 1969 (Social Work (Scotland) Act 1968).

It would seem that marital problems are most likely to be presented to social workers in the guise of general family problems, if at all. Ideally, and if social work staffing permitted, a visit to families before divorce could both offer support to single parents and provide a more accurate and professional assessment of the welfare of the children than is possible when, say, a grandmother gives evidence for the court. A somewhat similar suggestion was made by Eekelaar and Clive (1977, para 13.27), that a social worker should visit certain families, identified in some way before divorce, 'to see that the family is receiving proper social assistance and whether any further intervention is necessary in the children's interests'.

DEPARTMENT OF HEALTH AND SOCIAL SECURITY

Respondents who had had financial help from DHSS tended to look on it as no more than an entitlement. They measured it against their perceived needs and were grateful or indignant accordingly. The DHSS staff whom they saw were equated with the system which they operated and were seldom seen as individuals. In all, only twelve respondents (10 per cent of the sample), two men and ten women, said that Social Security had been helpful. Even for them, staff were seen as 'kind' if they gave grants for furniture or clothing.

DHSS visitors came in for a little more praise than the counter staff; several respondents had found them friendly but had not discussed any personal problems with them. Only one respondent, a 20 year old wife, said she had not liked her DHSS visitors, who were always men: 'Maybe it would have been different if it had been a lady'. One husband, with custody of his four children, had had three different women visitors but it was his fourth visitor, a man, who told him that he was entitled to a single parent benefit (probably the child benefit increase). 'I counted up and found we'd been done out of £2 a week so they put it up.'

Counter staff had seldom left enough impression for any comment to be made. Occasionally they were criticised. A 26 year old mother of three (of whom only two were her husband's) had felt ashamed when she was asked which father had fallen behind with maintenance payments. 'He made me feel very uncomfortable. He made it worse because he was younger than me.' A 33 year old wife had a more personal complaint. She was interviewed about her application for Legal Aid for divorce by a neighbour: 'I was embarrassed and felt he should have passed me on to someone else.' By coincidence, he had earlier been a customer in the bank where she worked and she had always deliberately avoided him, so that she did not have to know her neighbour's affairs. Few of the remaining 34 pursuers who had been Legally Aided made any comment about any assessment interview by DHSS staff. One husband who had later declined Legal Aid had been embarrassed by the questions asked at DHSS about his cohabitee's financial affairs.

Conclusion

DHSS was not normally seen as a potentially helping agency, since the staff were bound by statutory constraints and their discretionary powers were not understood.

HOUSING AGENCIES

There was considerable mobility among respondents during the period of separation. Only 30 (25 per cent) were still living in the marital home at the time of divorce, while 50 (42 per cent) were living, at divorce, in the home to which they had moved on separation. A further 40 (33 per cent) had made more than one move.

Before and after separation and at divorce, the respondents had lived as follows (listing the main home after separation for those who had moved several times).

TABLE 5.2   Type of Housing Before and After Separation and at Divorce

	Before separation %	After separation %	At divorce %
Local authority	51	17	27
Private sector (owned or rented)	42	27	35
In relatives' home	7	47	27
In friend's home	–	2	–
In new partner's home	–	7	11

Two wives who had been unable to leave their husbands because they had nowhere else to go had both approached Shelter but had been disappointed. 'I wanted to leave, but I had nowhere to go. It was then I needed help, but I couldn't find any. Just somebody advising me what to do ... I rang Shelter for a house, but they had no houses. I went to the Corporation for a house, but they wouldn't do anything.'

Relatives, but especially parents, had played an important part in helping to re-house separated spouses, either temporarily or permanently. Many respondents who had moved to their parents' homes, either with or without young children, had apparently made no effort to find alternative accommodation but had been content to stay where they were.

After divorce, only three husbands and two wives appeared to be dissatisfied with their housing. These husbands were fatalistic and said that they had little chance

of finding a new home as single men and had therefore not tried to do so; one wife
was continuing a long search for an exchange local authority tenancy in another
area. The only respondent who appeared to be positively unhappy with her housing
was a wife with a seven year old daughter, living in a bed-sitter.

Local Authority Housing

There had been twelve new local authority tenancies, to three husbands and nine
wives. Three of these wives had acquired tenancies after their husbands had left,
as a result of being on waiting lists during marriage. Four other wives had moved
first to relatives and then had had the original local authority tenancy transferred to them, with their husbands' agreement.

Only 18 respondents had applied to the local authority for housing and none had
considered the department to be helpful until they had been allotted a house.
Staff were faceless: a place on a waiting list was not appreciated and nor was the
offer of a house in an undesirable area.

A few wives had felt desperate when they had first left their husbands and had
trudged the streets looking for accommodation other than their own parents' homes.
By the time of divorce they had been rehoused by the local authority and their
difficulties had receded in their memories.

Four wives had consulted their district councillors as well as the housing department and were convinced that their subsequent rehousing by the local authority had
been the result of the councillors' intervention.

Private Sector Housing

Before separation, 50 respondents (42 per cent) had lived in private sector
housing: these were eight individuals (five marriages) in rented accommodation and
42 individuals (26 marriages) in owner occupied houses. Since both partners were
not interviewed in all of these marriages, it was not possible to measure the
total movement within the private sector.

Two respondents had continued to live in the rented marital homes, and two had
found other private accommodation to rent. Three had moved in with relatives and
one had bought a flat.

Ten respondents had continued to live as owner occupiers in the marital home; 18
had managed to buy new homes (nine husbands and nine wives); six had joined new
partners; four had moved in with relatives; two had acquired local authority
tenancies and two had found privately rented accommodation.

None of those living in the private sector during their marriages seemed to have
had rehousing difficulties. All but four of the house purchasers had been childless
and had had two incomes between the spouses. Only two in all (both halves of a
couple with two children) described a lowering of standards in housing.

Conclusion

Housing difficulties had not loomed large for most respondents. The readiness of
parents to take back their married children had often paved the way towards
adjustment as separated spouses.

CHAPTER 6

VOLUNTARY ORGANISATIONS

MARRIAGE GUIDANCE

The perceived need for a new organisation to provide counselling services for people faced with difficulties in their marriages led to the formation of the National Marriage Guidance Council in 1938 and the Scottish Marriage Guidance Council in 1947. It was believed that 'only a minority of people nowadays will turn naturally to a pastor or priest ... the doctor has neither the time nor the confidence', and that 'the decay of the close-knit family association' left many without traditional family support (Mace, 1948).

In 1947 the Denning Committee on Procedure in Matrimonial Causes recommended the formation of a marriage welfare service, to be sponsored by the state (but not to be a state institution). A year later the Harris Committee on Grants for the Development of Marriage Guidance (1948) recommended that government grants be given, for an experimental period initially, to support selection and training of marriage guidance counsellors and to contribute to the cost of administration. Some years elapsed before the Home Office, in consultation with the Department of Health and Social Security, set up a Working Party on Marriage Guidance, which published a consultative document, Marriage Matters, in 1979. The findings and recommendations did not refer to Scotland, but nevertheless had some relevance for the Scottish Marriage Guidance Council, which continues to be autonomous and to be financially supported by the Scottish Office.

Selection and training for marriage counselling has provided a body of highly skilled volunteers, but the volume of counselling in Scotland and in Edinburgh has not kept pace with the increased rate of divorce. In 1978, marriage counsellors saw one partner or both in 2177 marriages in Scotland, 475 of these being in Edinburgh. In the same year, 8447 divorces were granted in Scotland, including approximately 1300 divorces of couples with at least one partner living in Edinburgh (see Reid, 1979).

Lasch (1977) showed that social pathologists, marriage counsellors and psychiatrists have all in turn been criticised for imposing their own moral values on their clients. Marriage counsellors have attempted to show that their aim is to help their clients to work out their own solutions to problems in any relationships, but they find it difficult to change their reputation of being marriage savers.

Among the 120 divorced respondents, twelve (10 per cent) said they had been to
marriage guidance, five of them mentioning it as their immediate reaction to the
initial question. They were seven husbands and five wives, including both halves
of two couples. In addition, two out of twelve interviewed in the pilot survey had
been to see a marriage counsellor (both halves of one couple). By comparison, 13
per cent of Murch's petitioner sample had consulted a marriage counsellor (Murch,
1975).

The twelve marriage guidance clients conformed fairly closely to the whole sample's
pattern of age at marriage and at divorce, except that the husbands who had seen a
counsellor had a lower mean age at divorce than those who had not. But those with
and without marriage counselling experience diverged in two respects: de facto
length of marriage (i.e. to the date of final separation) and social class.

The marriage guidance clients emerged with a far shorter de facto length of
marriage: the two of longest duration were of 8 and 10 years and in both of those
(for both spouses and for one wife, respectively) counselling had been at an early
stage in the marriage. Hence, all those in the study who had seen a marriage
counsellor had done so within four years of marriage. One of these marriages had
lasted for rather less than three months, as had three others in the whole sample.

The marriage guidance clients were heavily and evenly weighted towards the upper
end of the social class scale compared with the others in the sample. This accords
with the social class distribution of clients seen by the local marriage guidance
council in 1972, the only year for which figures are available. Figures produced
for the silver jubilee exhibition of Edinburgh Marriage Guidance Council showed
that, in Edinburgh in 1972, 33 per cent of the clients were in social classes I
and II, compared with 26 per cent in the Edinburgh population in the 1971 census,
and 14 per cent of the clients were in social classes IV and V, compared with 25
per cent in that census.

Five of the ten couples (50 per cent) were childless, compared with 32 per cent of
the whole sample, but this reflects the higher proportion of childless respondents
in social classes I, II and IIIN in the whole sample.

Experience of Marriage Counselling

Only four of the twelve clients (two wives and one couple) had sought counselling
before deciding to separate. Six of the twelve (five husbands and one wife) had
been appreciative of counselling, mainly - so they said - for the opportunity to
talk. Only two of these six had had emotional support from their mothers.

Experiences and perceptions of counselling which were reported could have been
coloured by subsequent events and by eventual divorce. While most had expected to
find a sympathetic listener who gave positive advice towards saving the marriage,
a few had found something more. A wife aged 27 at divorce said 'they were quite
helpful ... It was a big decision (to separate) and I wouldn't say she (the
counsellor) encouraged it. But she certainly made a lot of things clearer.' This
wife had not expected the counsellor to provide any solution, but had felt the
need to talk things over and to understand what was going wrong. She had not confided in her parents, although she saw them regularly. Her husband's psychiatrist
had recommended that she should continue to see a marriage counsellor.

One couple had each seen the same counsellor about five times, always separately.
Both said that joint interviews had not been suggested (although joint interviews
are often given). The wife said that for three visits the counsellor mainly
listened, which she found helpful because she 'couldn't keep on about it to

friends; that's not part of a friendship'. On her next two visits, she told me,
she got very upset and the counsellor 'got angry and told me to pull myself
together – I don't think she knew how to handle it' and so this wife broke off
counselling when she no longer felt in control of it, while putting the blame on
the counsellor. Her husband had found the same counsellor to be 'totally detached'
and he had been helped to 'gather his wits'. In retrospect, he thought that he had
had mainly practical advice, 'to renew lost acquaintances and take up past
hobbies'. Both claimed that the counsellor had advised them to see less of each
other.

Another couple had both been disappointed. The wife told me 'they just wanted us
to sort of talk, and I felt we were able to do that at home without onlookers',
while the husband said 'it was insulting to one's intellectual intelligence to be
dealt with by amateur Freudian psychology'.

Another wife reported similar reactions: 'Basically it was just an ear. They sit
and listen. They couldn't give advice, or weren't prepared to give advice. They
direct their questions so that you think of your own answers.'

Several respondents saw counselling in terms of correcting an erring spouse. One,
who had 'tried marriage guidance' during an early separation, claimed 'the
counsellor didn't want to see me again; they concentrated on my husband'. Another,
a husband of 24, said his wife, 20, had gone once alone at his request to 'the
marriage council' and then several times with him. She was the first to break off
counselling, and he soon followed suit because 'she was the one at fault' and they
'were not getting anywhere'. He admitted it had been helpful to talk 'on my part,
but not on my wife's part'. He could not be specific and did not know what he had
expected from counselling. Although he had returned, for a while, to live with his
parents who had later given him practical assistance when he secured custody of
his two very young children, he had not wanted to talk to either parent about his
marriage. His wife denied that she had ever been to marriage guidance. These
expectations of counselling were similar to those of the dissatisfied clients in
Mayer and Timms' study, who had expected active support in correcting other
people's behaviour (Mayer and Timms, 1970).

One husband seemed to have been more impressed by the confidentiality than by the
counselling and said of the counsellors:

> They're trained, they're psychiatrists and intelligent
> people, very sympathetic and give you the amount of time you
> need. They're very discreet too and make sure as far as
> possible that no two people meet each other. If a woman or a
> man is worried about their marriage for any reason, there
> might be tremendous gossip if they were seen there ... They
> were totally understanding.

However, he saw his counsellor only twice and thought there was no point in
returning when his wife refused to make an appointment. He, also, had not spoken
much to his parents. 'My mother was no help. I did not use their shoulders
verbally ... My father understood completely that marriages are made and broken by
two people and I could cope.' On the other hand, he claimed to have had a great
deal of support from friends.

Respondents were not asked how they had heard of marriage guidance, but one man
had taken the advice of 'one bloke, in particular, at my work (who) went through a
divorce too and he had been there'. He laughed and said it hadn't helped him or
his friend – neither had got their wife back. He saw a counsellor three months
after his wife had left him: 'I explained the situation and they wrote to my wife.

It might have been useful if she'd gone. As it was, the whole exercise was a waste
of time ... It was all in confidence, and it was nice to talk it over quite
freely.' He had hoped to discover from the counsellor why his wife had left him.
She, in turn, had laughed when asked whether she had ever been to marriage
guidance: 'My husband phoned and told me he'd made an appointment for me. And my
Mum phoned me to say there was a letter for me - I told her to open it ... I
didn't want the marriage to work. The only thing I wanted to have was help over
whether I could claim for alimony.'

In the case of another couple, the husband had found, as he had expected, that it
was a relief to talk. 'They were very pleasant people, but it was too involved for
them to be able to do anything. It was a lost cause.' He had been surprised to be
told by his counsellor that his was 'quite a common situation, but it was out of
her (the counsellor's) control because my wife wouldn't co-operate.' He thought
that something like marriage guidance should be available for everyone but that,
at present, most people assume that anyone who goes there has a sexual problem.
After a marriage lasting for three months, he was conscious of this label being
attached to him in any case, although he did say 'it was mainly in me'. His wife
told me:

> when we were in the throes of all the problems, he suggested
> it and he went to a marriage guidance counsellor. He tried
> to persuade me, but I wouldn't go. I'm an independent strong-
> willed person. Basically, I think its a failure if you go to
> someone else for help. I wanted to solve our problems our-
> selves, but in the end we didn't.

She claimed that the counsellor had told her husband that she 'had never met anyone so bloody stupid as he was'.

Several of these perceptions of counselling came from people who were themselves
professionally involved in 'caring' and who might have been expected to have
understood what counselling would mean. They seemed not to have applied their own
professional knowledge to counselling when roles were reversed and they had become
clients. They appeared to have retreated from counselling as soon as they were
asked to look below the surface of their marriages. However, a hospital sister,
who had not seen a counsellor, said 'professional people don't use outside
agencies so much: they tend to use their own resources'.

Most of the 108 respondents who claimed not to have been to marriage guidance
offered no comment. Although none asked what it was, possibly some had not heard
of it, but 22 had something to say about it. Four husbands and two wives had
suggested counselling but had taken no action when their spouses had refused: 'I
asked him, years ago, and he said there was no point', 'six or seven years ago, I
suggested it to my wife but she wouldn't go ... no, I couldn't go myself, could
I?', 'he wouldn't go, and I felt it was no good if we didn't both go', 'she turned
it down flat and I didn't think there was any good out of going on my own'
(although he had been 'very conscious of the need of someone to talk to'), 'it's
all very well, but as far as marriage guidance is concerned, it's no good unless
you both go'. It was not clear whether these people thought that counselling was
not available for one spouse without the other, or whether they thought that it
could not help one alone. Both beliefs are unfounded in practice.

Some gave reasons for not seeing a counsellor: 'My husband was involved with someone else, and one person alone can't make a marriage work,' 'I knew what was wrong
with my marriage. Anyhow, they are simplistic. In terms of people I know there - I
don't want to sound arrogant, but the kind of advice they give would not have been
any use to me.' One wife had asked her doctor for a 'nerve tonic' and had been

advised to go to marriage guidance, but she told me 'I don't believe in it; if you can't sort out your own problems, no one else can.' None of them had considered that counselling might help them through a difficult period: all had seen it as a problem-solving service.

A wife who said 'I would rather talk to someone I knew' had been impressed before her marriage when, as part of a course on which her employer had sent her, she had spent an afternoon at a marriage guidance office in England: 'They were just ordinary people, from different professions, from all walks of life. And they just take donations.' She had not expected them to be so nice, she said: but she had still not wanted to approach her local council.

A childless husband, aged 27, had a suggestion to make:

> When we weren't getting on too well, we should have gone
> there ... Perhaps they should make it compulsory to see a
> marriage guidance counsellor. Even if you go along thinking
> it's a waste of time, perhaps they could pinpoint something
> that would help ... One couple I know went along and were
> helped ... Then, having tried marriage guidance and made
> sure the marriage is finished, they should make it as cheap
> and easy as possible to get divorced.

A less favourable picture was held by a battered wife of 22: 'At the marriage bureau they've been happily married, how the heck can they understand? ... I wonder how many marriage counsellors would turn round and say they think its better if you two split up.' She would have preferred a self-help agency similar to Alcoholics Anonymous, and thought that the CAB and Samaritans should have a 'list of names and addresses of people who could help because they've been through it'.

Conclusions

Marriage guidance was seen by almost all of the 10 per cent who had had experience of counselling and of the 18 per cent who offered their ideas about it to be a means of getting practical advice on how to restore a marriage in which the partners had already separated. It was a final resort for trying to save a marriage which had probably already died. Results, if any, were expected to be visible and quick. The concept of counselling or of examining personal relationships or feelings was probably alien to most of the 120 divorced people interviewed.

Advances made in counselling skills are of little avail if the number of clients falls in the face of a rising divorce rate. A public relations exercise is clearly required to sweep away myths and to attract many more clients.

CITIZENS ADVICE BUREAU

A total of 23 (19 per cent) respondents had consulted the Citizens Advice Bureau (CAB). There were 4 husband pursuers, 11 wife pursuers, 1 husband defender and 7 wife defenders. They were of all ages, but were evenly weighted towards the younger end of the age range.

Eight, or one third, of these CAB clients had asked only for the name of a solicitor, five of them going in person and three asking by telephone. Two others had telephoned to ask for an appointment with the CAB solicitor on duty. A further six were referred to solicitors after explaining their problems which ranged from

marriage difficulties to the division of property and advice (to a man) about
looking after a son. Some of these six had 'told them the gist' or 'told them the
position and they thought, rather than offer advice, they would give me the name
of a lawyer'. Three more had gone to discuss their marriages 'to see where I stood
about divorce before I went to a lawyer. They ... explained a lot, but there's
nothing you can do if your wife leaves you.'

Of the remaining four, three had had advice on quasi-legal problems and one had
gone to obtain a list of child-minders.

All but two had been satisfied with CAB services: one said she had been told to
return to her husband, and the other left in tears after apparently being advised
to put her children in a home until trouble with neighbours had blown over.

This CAB experience of divorced respondents seemed to indicate a preponderance of
legal problems; for instance, none had sought advice over housing or employment.
On the whole, the CAB seemed adequately to have fulfilled the role described by
Morris, Cooper and Byles (1973) as 'a place to go to find out where to go'.

OTHER ORGANISATIONS

Other voluntary organisations which were mentioned by respondents were Samaritans
(twice), Gingerbread (twice), Citizens Rights Office (once), a social club for the
divorced and separated (once), Alcoholics Anonymous (once) and local community
organisations (four times). One unemployed labourer had twice been to Samaritans
to discuss his pending divorce and his excessive drinking. He had also been to the
Citizens Advice Bureau and he differentiated between the two: 'You go to the
Citizens Advice if you want something done like getting a solicitor, but you go to
the good Samaritans if it's something to do with your life.' A young wife had
several times appreciated telephone support from the Samaritans shortly before
separation: 'I felt terribly alone. I'd be in this room and my husband would be in
bed asleep. I used to sit and cry. I felt completely and utterly alone. I needed
someone to talk to ... Just a voice.' The two who had been to Gingerbread had had
different needs, a wife wanting a new social life and a husband wanting information about welfare benefits: both had been satisfied. One husband had had a
visit from a member of Alcoholics Anonymous, who turned out to be someone he knew.
'I liked him and I knew he drank. I couldn't be as bad as that, I was thinking
when he left. There's no chance of me being an alcoholic' and the contact had not
been followed up.

Most had never considered approaching any other organisation for help, but two
were definite that they would never want to join an organisation of separated
people: 'I always picture them sitting moaning about their ex-husbands'.

CHAPTER 7

THE FAMILY

The Wolfenden Committee on the future of voluntary organisations (1978) said 'The help and support that family, friends and neighbours give to each other is so much taken for granted that it often hardly enters into the discussion of the provision of social services.' Some writers have reported the important role played by the family in giving support to its members.

Townsend described old people receiving help, practical and emotional, mainly from female relatives who lived either in the same household or nearby. He found that this help was often reciprocated and that the elderly, particularly the women, derived satisfaction from providing practical help for their married children or their grandchildren. This reciprocity was an important element in the pattern of care: if the elderly were unable to offer help, they were less likely to receive it (Townsend, 1957).

In a study of widowhood, Marris (1958) found that mothers, daughters and sisters gave far more regular help than friends or neighbours, but that the widows turned to their brothers for practical advice. Quarantelli (1960) demonstrated that the family has not, as is often suggested, lost its traditional supportive role. He studied accounts of behaviour after many community disasters and noted that 'the extended family is the major source to which disaster victims turn for help'.

The evidence collected in the present study emphasises the value of informal sources of help (and see Table 4.2).

Loneliness after separation ('just getting used to a different way of life') was an important element in the period of re-adjustment. It took by surprise some who had looked forward to a life without their spouse, but had not calculated what the loss of adult companionship would mean. Family and friends provided an important service in helping to combat loneliness and to assist in establishing a new social life.

A graphic account of the problem was given by a man of 32 who had agreed with his wife, after six years of marriage, that they should separate. There were no children, and he had continued to live in the matrimonial home, which he owned. At interview, fifteen months later, he admitted to feeling very lonely. 'Some days are OK, on others I am down. If I am in a good patch, I forget about it. If I stop to think, it gets bad'. He was not the only one to find that weekends were the worst time. Saturdays were worse than Sundays, because on Sunday he would soon be going back to work. Working days got bad at 4.30 or 5 p.m. as he realised another lonely evening was ahead. He looked around for something to do and found that housework, washing or ironing helped to fill the time. 'You don't get asked out. You feel awkward; probably your friends do too. There's something funny about going out alone.' He went out for a drink with a divorced colleague a few times, but felt uncomfortable. 'I don't want to go out with that kind of person. No, I don't quite mean that, because that's what I am.' Before the separation, for a while, he and his wife had both lived in the house but not together. They had seldom seen each other and had prepared separate meals, but in retrospect he realised that the situation had been less lonely, because of the knowledge that someone else was in the house.

Coming home from work to an empty house had been an unanticipated difficulty to be faced. A childless wife of 34 had felt desolate after nine years of marriage: 'Even watching TV it would be nice to have someone to discuss the programme with'. And a man of 40 had worried that he would die and no one would know. One wife's view was 'no matter how bad your marriage is, you're needed for washing, cooking and so on. Once you walk out, nobody needs you. You have to find a new purpose, especially if you walk out on your children and you find that they're surviving without you.'

PARENTS

Parents figured largely in the lives of many respondents, most of whom had a family network available which gave some kind of support during the period of separation. In the sample, 47 husbands (78 per cent) and 50 wives (83 per cent) had mothers; 38 husbands (63 per cent) and 41 wives (68 per cent) had fathers. One parent or both was instinctively mentioned first by 42 respondents (35 per cent) (19 husbands and 23 wives). Of these, 17 said 'parents', while 20 specified their mothers and five their fathers. Occasionally, they were the first to spring to mind, but had not been helpful. One husband, aged 27, when asked whether there was anyone in particular to whom he had turned, replied 'No; least of all not to my parents'. Nine (four husbands and five wives) of the 30 who claimed to have had informal emotional support from only one source had turned to their mothers.

Parental Attitudes to Marriage

In Scotland, there has never been a legal requirement to obtain parental consent to a marriage, and it has been possible since 1929 for young people aged 16 or over to marry without the approval of their parents. Previously, the minimum age for marriage, still without requiring parental consent, had been 14 for boys and 12 for girls. The Kilbrandon Committee on the Marriage Law of Scotland (1969) considered the arguments for introducing compulsory parental consent, and compared the divorce rates of young marriages in Scotland with those in England and Wales, where there had for many years been a legal requirement to obtain parental consent to civil marriages contracted under the age of 21. Since the divorce rate in England and Wales for these young marriages was higher than for similar marriages in Scotland, the Kilbrandon Committee concluded that there would be no advantage in introducing a legal requirement for parental consent to young marriages in Scotland.

It may be that some parents appear to give their approval to their children's marriages, realising that the marriages are likely to take place whatever they say. In that case, it might be preferable for parents to accept the inevitable and not to antagonise young couples at the start of their married lives by showing dis-approval.

Parents were said to have approved of the marriages of 45 husbands and 41 wives in the sample, although 10 of these husbands and 13 of these wives had reservations about this apparent approval. Parental disapproval was reported by 9 husbands and 17 wives. Six husbands and two wives either gave no information or had not had parents alive at the time of marriage.

Qualified approval could be 'they were not really bothered one way or another', but it was mainly expressed as a subsequent change of face: 'they didn't say anything very much; later, they admitted they had had misgivings,' 'I thought they approved at the time, but now I know they didn't really; I think they put a good face on it when we got married,' 'now they say no, but at the time they did'. It was perhaps easy for some parents to give support after separation by admitting to having had doubts about the marriage, saying 'Oh, I knew he wasn't right for you'. Some parents had reluctantly agreed to a marriage even when they clearly thought their son or daughter was too young. 'My Mum told me before I got married "you're too young; you may be 19 but you're not 19 up here"' (tapping her head). 'My father didn't say much. My mother would never stand in my way. She would never say don't.' A professional man's mother had not expected the couple to get on well together. She was 'not very keen. She could see it was not going to work, but you are not going to listen'.

While 26 (22 per cent) of the 120 respondents reported that their parents had disapproved of their marriages, it must be remembered that this was said with hindsight and may not have amounted to pleas not to marry, nor to any measure of real disagreement between the generations. Disapproval had usually been because the partners were thought to be too young or because the parents had not liked the prospective spouse but 'put up with him for my sake' or 'my mother never liked my wife'. Twice the disapproval had been on religious grounds. One Catholic wife had left her home in Ireland against her parents' wishes, and was married within six months to a non-Catholic whom she had known for three. A man married at 21 said:

> One of the reasons my parents disapproved was I was
> Protestant and my wife was Roman Catholic. I enlisted with
> a Roman Catholic priest but he became so adamant that his
> religion was the only true religion, we had a blazing row
> and I stormed out. Her mother thought I'd taken her daughter
> away from the true church.

One wife said her mother was possessive and would have disapproved of any husband for her 21 year old daughter.

Parental disapproval, as might be expected, had decreased with the age of the marriage partners and inevitably much of the disapproval was for those who had married under 20. However, only one of the seven men who had married aged 16 to 18 claimed parental disapproval of the marriage. Seven of the nine husbands whose parents had disapproved had been 19 to 21, at the time of marriage, the very young husbands having met with more approval. Social class had had no effect on parental approval.

Only one respondent volunteered that a premarital pregnancy had been the reason for her marriage. Her father had insisted that she get married at 16 because she was pregnant (and Catholic). She gave the impression that she had always blamed her father for a marriage which she had not wanted. 'Everybody was pleased about the marriage except me.'

Parental Attitudes to Separation and Divorce

Breaking the news of a separation to parents was sometimes anticipated with
trepidation because of perceived or imagined parental attitudes to marriage breakdown. Several respondents tended to think that their parents would be shocked,
especially if they did not often meet, but found that this was not necessarily so.
Two, whose parents lived abroad, had visited them to break the news. One of these
had tried to explain on the telephone but had lost courage. On her visit, she
found 'they were glad the marriage had ended; they seemed to have known more than
I realised'.

Among those who hesitated to speak to their parents were a fireman, who had been
grateful to his sister for telephoning his parents on his behalf, and a bus driver
who used to meet his mother for coffee in town and broke the news to her, but made
no attempt for a year after separation to visit his father. Two wives had tried
not to tell their parents that their marriages were rocky. 'I didn't like worrying
them at first. I felt I was making such a mess of my life.' However, this 39 year
old wife unexpectedly burst into tears when visiting her parents and had to tell
them that her husband was going out with another woman. And a wife of 33 said 'at
Christmas my father spoke to him because I was weeping all the time, but I didn't
tell them anything. I just hoped'.

A man of 25 did not tell his parents for six or seven months that his wife had
left him. 'Eventually I did tell my parents. They more or less said "I told you
so". It was difficult to tell them. They weren't too understanding over it.' The
wife from Ireland had never told her mother that she was separated, let alone
divorced, although the separation had lasted for three and a half years.

A clerk who had married at 20, found it extremely difficult to tell his parents,
three years later, that the marriage had broken down.

> It came as a total shock to them. My family hadn't been that
> much involved, and we only saw them every couple of weeks. I
> arranged to meet my mother somewhere neutral, to tell her. I
> think she thought I was going to start a family, so she
> couldn't believe it. She was very old-fashioned in that type
> of thing.

He had hoped that his mother would speak to his father, but she couldn't bear to
do so, so he did that too - 'my father's very much a working class man, and he was
very sympathetic and told me to get on with it'.

A number of respondents had been conscious that divorce was rare in their parents'
generation, and that a broken marriage in the family might be cause for shame or
embarrassment. 'They thought it should be for better or worse'. This view of
parental attitudes may have deterred some couples from separating even earlier
than they did. A woman of 50 said 'when I was small, divorce was a dirty word. But
I know now I should have got divorced when the oldest children were young. I
realise now it was a mistake not to have'. Some were relieved to find parents
unexpectedly sympathetic or understanding, and willing to take the burden of
explaining to others what had happened. Several found that their parents in turn
were relieved to hear the marriage was over, even although they had been initially
upset. A girl whose marriage had lasted for a year and a half said,

> For a while it was hardly mentioned. My husband and I had
> both hinted for a while that we weren't getting on ... I
> felt I had a very guilty conscience. My mother gave us the
> honeymoon and my father gave us the wedding - a big wedding.

So, after her husband had left her, she visited her family only occasionally. Nine
months later she came home to her parents, who said nothing about her having had
so much given to her to start off married life. This increased her feeling of
guilt.

At times, parents found it difficult not to put their own feelings first.

> My mother took it more badly. It was a status thing. The
> neighbours will talk, that sort of thing. But after two or
> three months they started not to bear a grudge, and by the
> time the divorce came through, they'd accepted it.

> It was quite a shock initially, as she had no inclination.
> My mother tried to be aware of modern views, but was
> restricted by her own. Her initial reaction was that it was
> a disaster, until she saw how comparatively easy it was for
> us.

More difficulties were reported with fathers than with mothers. 'My father was
more shocked than my mother.' 'My father believes that you should stick to a
marriage, whatever happens.' 'My Dad's old fashioned; he buries his head in the
sand. He's such a kind person, but he can't talk about things' - and this father
had never mentioned the separation but he no longer asked what shift his son-in-
law was working. One wife, loyal to her ex-husband, found her mother's attitude
the more helpful: 'My mother was more tolerant but not understanding; she didn't
quite understand what had gone on in my marriage. My father understood better, but
he was against my husband for all that he had done.' 'My parents were both disappointed at the marriage breaking up, especially my father' - this man had therefore found it easier to talk to his mother.

The parents who took the news badly could be persuaded through time that a
separation was for the best. 'They were very upset about it and tried to make me
change my mind, but they understood that I wouldn't.' Another mother had been
upset at first but had then 'agreed with my decision.'

A few had reason to know that their parents would dislike the idea of divorce. A
clerkess said that her parents had been shocked, especially as three of their four
children were now divorced: she saw her parents quite often, but her marriage and
divorce were never mentioned. One husband described his mother's ambivalence: 'My
father always took the line that it was up to me what I did, and he would support
me. My mother was more complicated, I suppose with conflicting feelings. She is a
conventional middle-class person, and thinks it is actually rather bad to have a
divorce.' His wife described his parents as 'a very rigid family. (The breakdown)
was a tremendous shock to his side. Given the way they used to be like, they had
relaxed a bit. They behaved very well, given the trauma over the years.' A wife
who was separated before her baby was born had not confided in her parents a great
deal. 'Probably they thought my situation was pretty unusual; they wanted us to
stay together'.

A wife from a very large family said:

> Mum was the last one to know about it. She and Dad had an
> awful lot of worries - at least, I suppose they must have
> had. My mother is a wee bit old fashioned, she thinks if
> you are married to a man, you should stay married for life.
> That's the type of woman she is. She doesn't believe in
> people living together. She was never a bad mother, you
> know, it's just her beliefs. Normally, it's your mother you

turn to, too.

Her father was: 'Just the opposite, and he came to see me every other week after
I had returned to this house.' Her mother told her never to come back and never
wanted to see her again because she was living with another man. However, one
brother died and she went to the funeral and back to her parents' house afterwards,
and her mother had been 'all right' since then. Her mother said 'I told you so'
because it hadn't worked out with this other man. 'In this day and age, they're
always wanting to say I told you so.'

One husband had not seen his father since he was ten years old; his mother died
before the separation, but he thought she would probably have been in favour of
the marriage breaking up. 'I had quite an easy time, not having parents around.'
He thought it must be 'an awful nuisance' to have parents trying to interfere.

Short marriages usually seemed to have caused little concern to parents, who
welcomed their married sons or daughters home again. The only report of intervention was in a separation after three months of marriage, which led to the
husband's mother trying 'to act as intermediary, to get us together by speaking to
my wife's parents. The negative reaction made her pretty bitter'. Yet his wife
said her parents also 'spent long hours trying to effect a reconciliation'. Five
other marriages which had lasted for less than a year seemed to have been un-
questioningly accepted by parents as broken down.

There were many warm tributes to parents, who were seen as the most obvious people
to whom to turn, and whose homes were seen as havens. 'If I hadn't had my Mum and
Dad, I wouldn't have got this far.' 'It was very comforting to be with them, and
they were very sympathetic.' 'If you've got your parents you can turn to, it's
awfully, awfully important. It depends what way you're brought up. We've always
been brought up to turn to our Mum and Dad.' 'If I hadn't had my family, I don't
know what I would have did. I think of people with nowhere to go, and they'd get
so lonely. I was very lonely when I first left.' Parental homes probably provided
more companionship, more amenities and less isolation than living alone.

Two wives realised that their mothers got some reciprocal satisfaction out of
being needed. A nurse said of her mother, 'She's almost too good, but I don't want
to offend her. She needs people to look after, to fulfil her.'

The need for a choice of supports was described as, 'There are some things you can
talk to your parents about and some things you can talk to other people about.'

Parents gave either practical help, mainly in the form of a home for those who had
left their spouses, or emotional support. The two were frequently not combined,
since respondents (especially men) who were happy to return to live with parents
often claimed that they had not then talked about their marriages. More husbands
(72 per cent) than wives (58 per cent) described practical help given by their
mothers, while similar numbers of husbands (58 per cent) and of wives (56 per cent)
had had practical help from their fathers. More wives (62 per cent) than husbands
(45 per cent) had had maternal emotional support, or paternal emotional support
(37 per cent compared with 26 per cent).

Accounts of how parents had, or had not, given support were of course given with
hindsight, and those who could say after divorce that they had not talked much to
parents after a separation two or three years earlier might have conveniently
forgotten what had happened. Their parents might have had different memories, and
have been conscious of a great deal of talking, listening, recriminations, or
advice given and ignored. If time had permitted, it would have been valuable to
have interviewed some parents.

It is difficult entirely to believe those husbands who said, as one did, 'I just came back and that was it.' A 24 year old lorry driver left his wife, baby daughter and father-in-law to live with his own father but insisted that there had been nothing to talk about. 'I didn't need anyone to talk to. It is one of those things that either it works or it doesn't, and it didn't work out.' An unemployed labourer 'supposed' his parents had helped him by giving him a home again. He 'just told them. I didn't want to talk about it, it was finished. It was time it came to an end, I didn't like it anyway. It was just a big bad dream. It was best to forget it.' He was only 20 and seemed to be relieved to be back among his seven siblings, but was surely also voicing a suppressed need to talk.

Practical Help

The younger the age at divorce, or the lower the social class, the more likely were parents to have given practical help. Nearly all husbands and wives whose de facto marriages had lasted for two years or less, had had practical help from their parents. For longer marriages, approximately half the husbands and half the wives had had practical help from both their fathers and their mothers, with one exception: 80 per cent of husbands married for four to ten years had had practical help from their mothers.

On separation, 21 husbands (35 per cent) and 18 wives (30 per cent) moved from the matrimonial home to their own parents' homes. Three of these husbands had been in prison but on release went to their parents since their wives had court orders to prevent them from returning. Between separation and divorce six more husbands and one wife moved in with their parents. Subsequently, eight husbands and thirteen wives left their parents again, so that at the time of divorce 20 husbands and 9 wives were living in their parental homes.

TABLE 7.1   Respondents who Lived with Parents after
                    Separation

	Husbands	Wives
Stayed on with parents after separation	1	3
To parents, on separation	21	18
To parents, during separation	6	1
Living with parents at some stage of separation	28	22
Left parents during separation and:		
Returned to matrimonial home	–	3
Moved in with new partner	4	1
Were allocated local authority house	1	6
Bought flat	1	3
Lodged with friend's family	1	–
Moved around, using parents as base	1	–
	8	13
Living with parents at divorce	20	9

The greater number of husbands living with their parents on divorce is, at least
partly, explained by the fact that many more wives than husbands kept the children
of the marriage and therefore had a claim to a local authority house, whether or
not the former matrimonial home. Other alternatives which might have been available
to these husbands were to go into lodgings or to live with other relatives. It was,
perhaps, surprising that only four men out of 28 had left their parents in order to
live with a new partner.

A further four wives and one husband had been offered homes with their parents but
had preferred to be independent. Most had lived in owner-occupied homes during
marriage; two had remained in the matrimonial home and two had bought another home.

Most of those who had returned to their parents had assumed that their previous
home was still available to them and, indeed, that they had a right to return. They
also looked at their own situation in terms of lack of choice: 'I came home, there
was nowhere else' and 'I had no money and nowhere else to go'. It did not,
apparently, occur to any of them that their parents might not welcome them back or
might prefer to live independently of their adult children. Some respondents did
not consider that their parents had helped them merely by giving them a home again.
Others had been actively encouraged by parents to return to the bosom of the family
and to have their wounds licked. These parents were saying, in effect, 'I told you
so'. Mothers who had reluctantly untied their apron strings hastily tied them
again.

The nine wives who lived with their parents at divorce were all under 30, but the
20 husbands were spread over the age range 20 - 43, including three in their 40s
(one of these with a young son). It would have been interesting to have discussed
with the parents of these last three their feelings about giving a home to their
middle-aged sons, and about any reciprocity of help.

The de facto length of marriage of those living with parents at divorce was similar
for husbands and for wives, the shorter marriages being more likely to have
returned to their parents.

The social class of those living with parents was III to V, with the exception of
one husband in social class II. Between a third and a quarter of each social class
III, IV and V lived with their parents at divorce, but this must be seen in the
context of greater childlessness in social classes I and II, most of whom also
lived in homes which they owned.

Some parents suffered overcrowding when they took back their married children. A
few already had other children and grandchildren living with them, so that beds had
to be shared and some members of a family might sleep in a living room or on a
floor. Respondents volunteered that their siblings had not complained about such
overcrowding, but none mentioned parental reactions.

By the time of the divorce, two husbands (out of ten with custody) and four wives
(out of 31 with custody) had established a new home for their children, as well as
themselves, with their parents. They had had considerable help from their parents
in caring for these children. All obviously intended to continue living with their
parents indefinitely, although a 42 year old husband thought that he would move out
when his son entered his teens. Others who had taken children initially to their
parents' homes had moved away to a newly allocated local authority house or back to
the original matrimonial home.

The two husbands mentioned were employed and needed their parents' assistance in
looking after the children. Two of the four wives had very recently started full-
time employment, with children aged 6 and 2 respectively. They each had only one

parent, previously living alone, who may have reciprocated an appreciation of company.

Most of the respondents who had taken their children temporarily to their parents' homes did not specify any particular help apart from having a roof over their heads.

Very few separated spouses who had not lived with their parents for all or part of the separation mentioned parents watching their children during working hours or the evening. A wife whose parents lived twenty miles away, was pleased that they had offered to have her four children for a week's holiday. Another wife had two small children, the younger one severely handicapped, and her mother had care of the older one, aged 5, during school term. This wife could have made her home with her parents, but would not then have had easy access to hospital and special school. She and her mother visited each other with both children, for a week at a time, and she thought that the five year old was quite happy about the arrangements, but was 'spoiled of course'.

Only four people, two men and two women, described financial assistance from their parents: a factory worker's mother had helped him to pay off arrears of rent but not two outstanding loans; a doctor's father had given money and access to a book account; a woman secondary school teacher and a hairdresser's receptionist had had financial support from parents but did not give any details. A few had indignantly denied that they had needed any 'help', initially interpreting this as meaning financial help.

Ten respondents had appreciated other practical help from their parents. One father had helped his son to decorate a newly purchased flat and another had accompanied his somewhat fearful daughter 'to collect my stuff' a fortnight after she had left her husband. Three sets of parents had helped with the process of selling a matrimonial home. A husband said that his 'mother came in handy for the likes of washing clothes'. Another husband spent a week with his mother, 'but I couldn't stand living with her'. When he then lived alone, he was happy for his mother to clean his house, do his washing and his messages and pay his bills in his absence. Finally, three had been extremely grateful for gifts from their parents: two childless wives had been given cars, and a father with two young children had been given a cassette recorder to compensate for lack of a social life: he thought that other parents might consider making similar gifts, to combat loneliness.

Two husbands whose parents lived in England had each had a long visit from their parents: one for two months, to keep house and look after the children while he looked for a smaller house; and one for a fortnight after his sister had phoned to tell their parents of the marriage break-up: both had been very glad to have their help and also to be able to talk to them while they suffered the initial shock of their wives' departure.

Emotional Support

Nearly half of the husbands and three fifths of the wives who had mothers alive and accessible had had some kind of emotional support from them.

An examination of their circumstances shows that husbands were slightly more likely than wives to have had emotional support from their mothers if they were aged 30 or less at the time of divorce. For those who were older at divorce, wives (74 per cent) were significantly more likely than husbands (24 per cent) to have found their mothers emotionally supportive.

Similarly, marriages lasting for four years or less led to a nearly equal chance of maternal emotional support for husbands and for wives. Longer marriages led to significantly more support for wives (66 per cent) than for husbands (27 per cent).

The higher the social class, the more likelihood was there of mothers having been emotionally supportive: this was particularly so for husbands.

Only one quarter of husbands (26 per cent of 38) and just over one third of wives (37 per cent of 41) had had emotional support from their fathers. Both husbands and wives were more likely to have had paternal emotional support after short marriages or if they were under 30 at divorce.

It might have been expected that parents who had not approved of their children's marriages would not have been willing to give emotional support when those marriages broke up: this might be so if the disapproval had been partly based on poor relationships within the family, with the two generations not getting on well together. If, on the other hand, parents had disapproved partly because they were sorry to see their offspring leaving home, then they might have welcomed them back with open arms and given a great deal of encouragement. In fact, a minority of husbands and a majority of wives whose parents had approved of their marriages had been conscious of emotional support from their mothers. The opposite held for those whose parents had disapproved of their marriages: a majority of husbands and a minority of wives had had this support.

Those who had had the closest contact with parents were those who had made their permanent homes with them. These were twenty husbands and nine wives. They were in a position to have had tremendous emotional support if it had been offered and acceptable.

Parental approval of the marriage was more evident among the husbands who had returned to live with their parents than among the wives. Although 70 per cent of the husbands living with parents at divorce had met with approval (or qualified approval) of their marriages (compared with 75 per cent of all husbands in the sample), only 56 per cent of wives living with parents had had such approval (compared with 69 per cent of all wives).

Most men living with parents appeared to have been swallowed up by a continuation of the life they had left. They did not question their acceptance and many did not see it as being supportive. A gas fitter, 22, said of his homecoming 'my mother was all for it'. Few husbands were as vocally appreciative of their parents as wives were.

Wives were able to admit slowly regaining confidence as they gradually talked to the parents with whom they lived. In particular, three whose de facto marriages had been short (three to nine months) had been surprised and grateful that their parents had not blamed them nor tried to dissuade them from ending such short marriages.

In the whole sample of 120, the one who appeared to have suffered most (mentally and physically) was a girl who, at 19, went through a severe depression and had a miscarriage after a violent marriage which had lasted for less than three months. Three years later she was able to describe most vividly the life-giving support from her parents. Her mother had looked after her at home, although hospital had been suggested by the family doctor.

> All I wanted to do is sit. I got to the stage when my Mum
> had to drag me upstairs to wash my face and my hair. If you've
> got someone who's going to sit and listen, you need them to

> take a firm hand at the time. I couldn't sleep at night. I
> used to sleep half the day and then sit and cry. I realise
> now how much they helped me. I thought they should be sorry
> for me. It upset them more to have to shout at me than it
> upset me when they shouted at me ... I don't know how I'll
> ever repay my Mum. She was with me for 24 hours a day. We've
> always been a close family. I never really bothered about
> anyone outside the family.

Her parents took charge of her sleeping pills and 'nerve pills'.

> They were afraid I'd take them all one night. I felt no one
> really cares for me, because they're shouting at me. There
> was no point of going on because no one cares for me. I felt
> suicidal. Then I started shouting back and Mum said to Dad
> "she's definitely getting better".

Two months after separation, 'I woke up one morning. I remember it as clear as a
bell.' She went downstairs and asked her mother to make her an appointment at the
hairdresser.

> My Mum was struck dumb. I don't know what done it. I decided
> he wasna worth it. It was like fighting back. I won't say you
> get over it. On my first wedding anniversary I had a good cry.

But her second anniversary passed without her noticing it. It took her the whole
of these three years to get back on her feet and to gain the courage to start a
new life, on her own and without her parents.

Many respondents could not differentiate between their parents when describing the
support given, but some had had a distinct preference for one parent, where two
were available. An apprentice plumber, married at 16, whose marriage had ended
after eighteen months, said 'My mother was more helpful than my father, but everybody would rather talk to their mother than their father.' When his mother died he
did not want to continue living in the parental home, but he found that his father
became easier to talk to after his mother's death. Another husband said 'These
things are usually left to a mother; my father took a back seat.' A barmaid had
been able to talk more to her mother who had not liked the marriage breaking up;
she could not talk to her father, in spite of the fact that he was glad when the
marriage came to an end, having disliked his son-in-law.

A wife of 26 had not felt willing to talk to her mother until after recovering
from an overdose, taken because of her unhappy marriage. She was sad that she had
had no support from her father, with whom she had not got on for many years; when
she was with him, tempers got frayed and he'd say 'no wonder your husband's not
living with you'.

Fathers no Substitute for Mothers

One third of those who had been emotionally supported by their mothers had
received similar support from their fathers; but where mothers gave no emotional
support, only 11 per cent had had support from their fathers. Even when mothers
had not been available, only 17 per cent had been supported emotionally by their
fathers instead.

Practical help was almost entirely given by both parents or by neither, where both
were available. Only 6 per cent of those who had had no practical help from their

mothers had been helped by fathers instead, although the absence of a mother had
more often led to helpful fathers.

These figures can be explained because practical help by either parent was usually
in the form of housing, and therefore was given by both parents or by neither,
where both were available. The part played by fathers was often a passive one.

Those who had had no maternal emotional support (whether or not they had mothers
available), and who had not turned instead to fathers who were available, had few
distinguishing characteristics. They were 19 husbands and 16 wives, spread over
the whole age range and the range of marriage duration.

Those few (four husbands and five wives) who had been emotionally supported by
fathers but not mothers, tended to be younger, to have had short marriages and to
be in social classes I or IIIM (the highest of the non-manual and of the manual
classes).

An indication that fathers' emotional support was experienced mainly to supplement
mothers', was the finding that all who had been supported by both parents (16, or
24 per cent of those with two parents) also had had other sources of support and,
indeed, had had nearly double the mean number of sources of emotional support (4.9,
the mean being 2.6). They seemed to use their fathers because they used most
available sources. A higher number, 27 (40 per cent) of those with two parents had
had no emotional support from either; this included three out of five husbands and
eight out of 16 wives with custody of their children. This would seem to contra-
dict Bott's suggestion that parents find it easier to divorce when they themselves
have parents to whom they can turn for support (Bott, 1957).

Contact with Parents

One unemployed husband and eight wives mentioned that they frequently saw their
parents although they did not live with them (but four of the wives had done so
temporarily). Three of these wives had moved home to live on the same stair as
their parents, thus gaining a mixture of support and independence which suited
them well.

One wife had been deserted by her husband immediately after she lost the unborn
baby for whom she had longed. Not surprisingly, she felt suicidal and leaned
heavily on her mother, who spent a great deal of time with her. She usually phoned
her mother from work during the day, and her mother visited her in the evenings
and also took charge of tablets prescribed. She could not face the short walk from
her office to her mother's house. She was 'absolutely petrified of the traffic. I
often had the feeling I'd like to walk into the traffic; I felt safer in a bus
going to my own home'. She added, 'If I hadn't had Mum, I'd have wanted to talk to
someone else. There must be thousands of females, and perhaps males too, who
haven't a mother to go to.' She felt more secure once she had moved next door to
her mother.

Another wife was able to lodge two of her children downstairs with her mother,
with whom she spent much of the day. Another had first taken her children to live
with her father, whom she had always found easy to talk to. When the local
authority flat above his became vacant, she managed to get the tenancy 'so that I
could keep an eye on my Dad, as he's a pensioner'. She and her father were in and
out of each other's houses and a support to each other. She felt 'safe' when he
sat in for her once a fortnight, which was as often as she could afford to go out.

The others who often saw their parents all lived across the road or down the road

from them. One wife, with two small children and a part-time job, saw her parents
on most days and another, with one child and no job spent a lot of time with her
mother. A childless wife had lived for a short time with her mother who 'gave me
a great deal of support. I could just retreat from everything and have everything
done for me'. After moving a short distance away from her mother, she still
appreciated this support.

There were some who had stood back, not wanting to worry their parents. A professional man of 36, shattered when his wife walked out, 'didn't want to spoil my
parents' holiday and did not tell them till they returned. There was nothing they
could do, and my mother would have worried.'

Other reasons were given for not leaning on parents. 'My father's been super, but
he's not the sort of person to pour out your heart to' and 'my mother wouldn't
understand, she's very conventional. She was a nuisance more than anything.' But
this mother had not been given an opportunity to understand, since she did not
know that her daughter and son-in-law had lived together for six years before a
marriage which lasted for a further four years.

The few who had not told their parents of their separation or divorce lived at
some distance from them and had virtually lost touch during their marriages, so
that there was nothing significant in not communicating with them - apart from the
Catholic wife who, while admittedly a poor correspondent, still did not want to
upset her elderly mother in Ireland.

Only two, both husbands, seemed to have felt obscurely let down by parents in
spite of frequent contact with them. A husband of 29 said 'I didn't go to anyone
for help'. Pause. 'I went to my parents. I was kind of mixed up myself, but they
said it wasn't their business, sort of style: they stated that to me. They wanted
nothing to do with it, so I accepted it.' A bank clerk of 32 had explained the
situation to his parents who 'were very upset about it and tried to make me change
my mind, but they understood that I wouldn't'. Neither of these husbands had
apparently again discussed their marriages with their parents, but had returned to
live with them.

Parents Present at Interview

Seven of the twenty husbands living with their parents, as well as one other
husband and two wives, were unfortunately interviewed in the presence of one
parent or both. All were asked whether they would prefer to talk in private either
at that time or at some other time. None accepted that suggestion and most said
they had no secrets from their parents, and were willing to have them present at
the interview. Two men obviously expected their mothers to disappear, as their
fathers had tactfully done, and were annoyed that a natural curiosity delayed
their departure.

One mother joined us, sat down to listen, answered the next question herself, and
was sharply told 'the lady's asking me the questions, mother' which effectively
silenced her, but may possibly have inhibited him. In the other case, the father
put on his coat and left the house. The husband-respondent, aged 43, invited me to
sit by the fire and turned down his mother's offer also to go out, saying he had
nothing to hide. His mother pottered about, in and out of the room, obviously
intensely interested. She interrupted when it came to questions about the teenage
children of the marriage. He changed his mind: 'Mother, are you going out? The
lady's talking to me' and, later, 'Is the lady interviewing you or me?' This was
an unhappy man, on the edge of tears throughout the interview. Several times,
showing signs of distress, he asked whether he had to continue with the interview,

and each time was assured that he need not. He did not take the offered opportunity
to terminate the interview or to postpone it to a time when his mother would not be
present, but masochistically insisted on continuing. Possibly the ordeal was
cathartic for he bade me goodbye with a pat on the shoulder, saying 'I like you.
God bless.'

Conclusions

Clearly, parents were of key importance to a large number of these divorced people,
among whom there had been little geographical mobility at or during marriage. Most
had lived in Edinburgh throughout their lives, so that their parents, if alive,
were easily accessible. All were asked whether they had lived near their parents
after marriage, but the replies were too disparate for analysis. It was interesting
that several denied being near parents who lived within two or three miles but were
not considered to be near enough for frequent visiting. For some, 'near' could only
mean round the corner or at least in the same housing scheme. Possibly the proximity of parents had played a part in breaking up some of the marriages, but no
evidence was collected on that score. Possibly the apparent willingness of parents
to take back their married children made it easy to break off a marriage. For both
husbands and wives, mothers were the most important source of informal emotional
support. Fathers and mothers both gave a great deal of practical support, mainly
in the form of housing and of looking after respondents' children.

IN-LAWS

Fifteen respondents (12.5 per cent) had been glad to continue some contact with
their in-laws after separation. These were six husbands and nine wives, most of
whom also had their own parents within reach. Where two parents-in-law were
available, wives had more often kept in touch with their mothers-in-law than with
their fathers-in-law. Propinquity was not a necessary factor, since some had kept
in touch by writing. A few had been more conscious of giving support to their
parents-in-law than of receiving it.

Some had felt a closer affinity with their parents-in-law than with their own
parents, and indeed several said that their parents-in-law were more sympathetic
towards them than to their ex-spouses, who were perhaps blamed for breaking up
the marriage. It seemed possible that some parents-in-law had felt some guilt for
their own child's behaviour in contributing to marital breakdown.

Emotional support was given to 7 of the 97 who had mothers-in-law and to 3 of the
88 who had fathers-in-law. Emotional support from both parents-in-law and
practical help from fathers-in-law tended not to duplicate the same from parents,
but mothers-in-law who gave practical help did so only where mothers did the same.

A woman divorced at 34, after eight years de facto marriage, said 'my mother-in-
law is still a good friend. She takes my part more than his. She knew all that
was going on. My parents didn't. I could talk to her quite a lot about it.' She
said that her husband did not see his family much: 'I think they're against him
for divorcing me' (although she had divorced him for adultery). Her husband told
me that he had not talked to his mother about his marriage, apart from explaining
the procedure of divorce. He had not felt the need to discuss anything more with
her, he said.

Another wife had turned to her mother-in-law, after seven years of marriage, and
had found it easy to talk to her. Her mother-in-law had said that if the marriage
were not going to work, it was better to part. This wife continued to write fort-

nightly to her mother-in-law, who did not live within easy reach, but was nevertheless more accessible than her own parents, who were abroad.

A husband whose wife had left him for another man, after 16 years of marriage, said
'I went to see my in-laws every week. They were very sympathetic. He tried to get
us back together. He went to see his daughter after I went back to the house ...
He didn't like the other man. My mother-in-law was very sympathetic too.' He lost
touch with his parents-in-law after they had failed to persuade his wife to return
to him. He had had no sympathy from his own parents, and had never got on with them,
before, during or after the marriage.

It had been comforting for some to cling to the knowledge that their parents-in-law
did not attach blame to them for the break up of the marriage. 'They knew it wasn't
my fault,' said a man of 26 whose wife had three years earlier found a new partner,
who had then taken his place in the home which he had left. A typist had found out
a few months after marrying at 21 that her husband had a girlfriend. She had felt
shattered; she had not wanted the marriage to end, although she had been so hurt,
but she and her husband had then lived separate lives in their flat until he moved
out to his parents' home. 'I still saw them both after my husband went to live with
them. They wanted me to visit them all the time. I think they felt very sorry for
me because there was another girl involved in my case.' She thought her parents-
in-law felt less guilty if she visited them, but she soon stopped going. She still,
four years later, met her husband's brother's wife occasionally, and had talked
more to her than to her own parents or to any of her eight siblings.

Most who described themselves as still friendly with their mothers-in-law had been
married for more than seven years and some for considerably longer. Two men who
'got on well' with their parents-in-law said they had been able to discuss any
problems with them.

Two wives had not felt able to meet their mothers-in-law after the separation,
although they would have liked to have done so. One, aged 42, corresponded
regularly with her mother-in-law who had always been a good friend but lived in
England. 'I couldn't face going to see her. There are too many memories. (My
husband) has a guilty conscience. He's never got around to telling her.' She said
her husband had not seen nor written to his mother since he left his family. He
just sent cards for birthday, Christmas and Mother's Day. Loyalty to her husband
had prevented the wife from telling her mother-in-law that another woman was
involved.

The other wife, aged 31, had had continuous and daily support from her own mother,
but also 'I was very close to my mother-in-law, and it hurt me not being able to
go and see her. I haven't seen her for two years. I can't bring myself to visit
her ... You've got me thinking.' She and her mother-in-law had continued to exchange birthday and Christmas cards, and a brother-in-law had already put out
feelers about her visiting again, so possibly she will pick up this friendship
again.

Two husbands had continued to value friendships with siblings-in-law. One used to
meet his wife's sister's husband twice a week; and the other had, for about twenty
years, looked on his wife's youngest sister as his own sister and had greatly
valued being able to make frequent visits to her and her family. 'It was a good
job she flitted up here.' One wife claimed to have only two friends, one being a
neighbour and one her husband's brother's wife.

It could be unfortunate if the loss of a spouse also meant the loss of a second
family. Fear of rejection inhibited some of those who had been close from making
conciliatory gestures. A young wife said, of her in-laws, after an eight month

marriage, 'I've not seen them at all. They're very nice people. I met my mother-in-law in the street once, and she started speaking. And his grandmother stopped me once when I hadn't even seen her.'

A bus driver, whose wife had taken his baby son away from him, said of his in-laws, 'If they come on my bus, they speak to me, and ask how I'm getting on. They're missing me. They're sorry it ended, but they say she made her bed and she must lie on it.'

'They act as though nothing had happened' was the plaint of some respondents, who visited their in-laws or happened to meet them in the street. 'They never ask how I'm doing or if I've heard from him.' Skirting round a potentially sensitive subject, it was easier just to pass the time of day with impersonal conversation. At the same time, these respondents did not seem to have made any conscious effort to disperse any embarrassment themselves.

Five wives and two husbands had kept in touch, often tenuously, with their parents-in-law for the sake of small children.

> Before I got my divorce, I used to take B. down to see Nana,
> that's my husband's mother. We got on OK. I thought she
> should see her granddaughter, but I don't know how she'd
> feel towards me now.

> My in-laws and my sister-in-law all helped. Well, not really
> helped, but we go to tea there and they come here for tea,
> and obviously the children enjoy going there and seeing
> their grandparents ... Sometimes, when we go, the children
> wonder if Daddy'll be there but I don't think he visits them
> at all.

A 27 year old wife said:

> I see my in-laws once a month in a very formal way. They're
> in their seventies and there's no need to deprive them of
> their grandchildren. There's not a great closeness, but I
> feel it wasn't their fault.

Some parents-in-law sent birthday presents to their grandchildren, but did not visit them. This seemed to satisfy the parents who had custody. Others gave presents to grandchildren who visited their father at their grandparents' home. This, too, was appreciated by wives who could not afford to buy any extras for their small children. It was rare for grandparents to visit a son-in-law or daughter-in-law, but one husband, with custody of four children, reported that his parents-in-law 'used to come quite a bit at first, especially their Grandad used to come on Sundays with lollipops'.

Two wives and a husband, all of whom had custody of children, had in-laws who took the children off their hands for a night or a weekend, or even for a week's holiday in Spain. Another wife, whose husband was in prison, had a teenage daughter who left home to live with her paternal grandmother to escape from her mother's requests to tidy her room or wash her clothes. But the grandmother could not control the girl, who returned to her mother after finding that her grandmother gave her presents but expected her to help in the house.

It was unusual to disapprove of either the contact or lack of contact offered by in-laws. Most were content with the situation. But one young wife with two small children was resentful that her in-laws had 'not shown any interest in the children and have not even sent birthday cards or Christmas cards. It was no fault of the children and that put my back up.' Another wife, aged 22, felt the opposite and had been cross that her husband's sister had come up with Christmas presents, which had reminded her two children of their father, when she thought they should forget him. She later phoned her mother-in-law and said she'd prefer her not to see the children again. 'She wasn't too pleased and said "I love the children as much as you".'

Only three wives had found their mothers-in-law to be antagonistic after the separation. 'My mother-in-law was very bitter towards me for what I'd done to her son' (leaving him after three months). And 'My mother-in-law blamed me. She knew what her son was like. Before I left him, she told me over the phone that he was my responsibility ... (I saw her) just once, across the street. Poor soul, she looked ten years older.'

Inevitably, some had never got on well with their parents-in-law, who were blamed for breaking up the marriage. 'My mother-in-law never liked me. She wouldn't like any girl that took her son away. She tried to break up the marriages of all three of her sons, and has succeeded with two divorced and one separated.' A 20 year old husband had spent the year and a half of his marriage in the home of his wife's parents who 'never stopped interfering'. He was rueful that the possibility of some privacy in the marriage had been nearly in his grasp. Two months after he had left his wife, she was allocated a house across the road from her parents, but she refused to take him back, and her parents forbade him to visit his baby son.

Other couples had started married life with the parents of one or the other, but had survived long enough to have their own house. It would have been interesting to know whether the lack of privacy at the start of a marriage had played much part in its eventual breakdown.

One family had what seemed to be curious living arrangements. At divorce, the husband lived with his divorced father-in-law while the wife and children lived further up the same stair. The husband claimed that he got on well with his father-in-law but he was emphatic that they had never discussed anything to do with the marriage. He asked to be interviewed on the common stair, since his father-in-law might overhear anything said in the house.

Future In-Laws

Few had anything to say about their new partner's parents, apart from the comment that a broken marriage did not recommend itself as an introduction to a proposed son- or daughter-in-law. Only one respondent had cause to be grateful to his future in-laws, who had sold a house at slightly below market price to him and their daughter, as a home for them and his children by his first marriage.

Conclusion

While there was some slight evidence to support the common belief that mothers-in-law often contribute to marital breakdown, there were more than enough accounts of good relationships with mothers-in-law to redress the balance.

SIBLINGS

Respondents who gave their number of siblings (two were not asked) had an average of 2.7 siblings each.   Twelve had none, 83 had one to four and 23 had five to twelve siblings.

Of the 106 who had siblings, 74 (70 per cent) had one or more sisters and co-incidentally the same number had brothers. These figures include many who were overseas or elsewhere in Britain and not easily accessible. However, some gave support by telephone or visits and therefore it was not possible to aggregate those who had siblings readily available. The numbers available to provide any kind of support were reduced by a good many who were thought to be too young.

The help given to 33 respondents by their sisters could be described as emotional support in 14 cases, practical help in 10 and both in a further 9. Brothers gave emotional support to 11, practical help to 8 and both to four; two also gave professional advice, since they were solicitors.

Six respondents (two husbands and four wives) quoted sisters as the first source of help, but none quoted brothers.

Emotional Support

Emotional support from sisters was given to 33 per cent of those who also had this support from mothers: where either the mother was not supportive or where there was no mother, those having emotional support from sisters dropped to 9 per cent.

Similarly, support from brothers was given to 17 per cent of those with support from mothers but to only 4 per cent of those with no mothers. Clearly, the lack of a mother or a mother's support did not lead to leaning on siblings instead.

Young and Willmott (1957) found that relationships with siblings were, to a large extent, determined by relationships with mothers. They found that daily contact between women and their sisters in East London was halved by the mother's death. Families without a mother had no focus and no reason to see each other so often.

The figures illustrate the comparative numbers of those who turned to parents or to siblings, but do not show the quality of support provided. Many had spoken with warmth and enthusiasm about their parents, but there seemed to be a more lukewarm attitude to siblings, whose support had often been of a transitory nature. A total of only seven - all women - had leaned heavily on siblings. Apart from one brother, these were sisters who had been especially supportive. Adams (1968) found in his urban American respondents that relationships with siblings were based more on interest in, and comparison with, each other than on the concern which char-acterised relationships with parents.

Wives were considerably more likely than husbands to have found their siblings supportive. Emotional support from sisters was given to 18 per cent of those husbands and to 46 per cent of those wives who had sisters. Emotional support from brothers was given to 16 per cent of those husbands and to 24 per cent of those wives who had brothers. Wives in this study had had more emotional support from siblings than the widows in Lopata' study (1978), where only 10 per cent had felt able to turn to siblings for support in crises. She found little evidence of emotional support for widows from any relatives other than parents or children.

A young wife had appreciated one brother's support more than that of her other six siblings. He was the one nearest to her in age. She had returned to her parental home after a brief but violent marriage and had been supported by all her family through a severe depression. Although her brother 'joked about it; at the time I didn't laugh at it', she had found his acceptance of her condition to be thera-peutic. 'My sister would never talk about it. She was frightened in case she upset me.' Instead, this sister and her husband 'bought me quite a lot of clothes' as their contribution to a slow rehabilitation. The brother had not only been more understanding, but he and his wife had cajoled the young girl into starting to go out again, and into making the beginnings of a new social life.

Another wife had been in a similar situation, returning to the family home after a brief marriage, so that siblings were readily available.

> My sister had a very good ear, and a shoulder to cry on. A married couple who have been very great friends for a number of years were the same. Between the three of them, they managed to get me to talk about it. My sister and my friends forced me to talk about it and to go out. I spent a lot of time refusing invitations from my sister and her fiancé if anyone else was going to be there too. And I wouldn't go to my friends if anyone else would be there.

Eventually, her hand was forced:

> The four of them said if I didn't go to a party with them, that was the end of the friendship. I suppose that was the first step.

She had believed their threat, and her sister's insistence paid dividends in starting her recovery. 'For a long time after that, I did accept invitations but, come time to go, after I had been sitting at home for two hours (i.e. after returning from work) I always regretted it.'

Those whose sisters had cushioned the shock of a broken marriage had ranged in age from 23 to 41 at divorce. One of them had taken her baby to live in her father's house and they had had to share a bedroom with her unmarried sister. 'Crying at night made for tension, but if it hadn't been for my sister, I would have gone off my head, it was such a distressing time.' When they disagreed (for instance, the wife liked to sleep with the window open, and her sister with it shut), 'my sister used to count to ten, while I just let fly.' Having expected to live with her father and sister for only a short time, she had stayed for 17 months, and her sister had obviously played an important part in putting her back on her feet after the shock of being turned out by her husband. During the marriage and again after those 17 months, she had lived near her sister and their elderly father. The sister had also contributed financially by paying for furniture to be stored and 'I still have to depend on my sister by letting her clothe my son.'

Some had had several sisters but had turned to one rather than to the others. 'My big sister has been a real help. I put on an outward show, though I was cut to pieces. She offered to take me into her house at any time, but I'd never run back to anyone like what he done, going back to his Mammy.' She seldom saw her other two sisters, but saw enough of one to say 'I'd never stay with my wee sister. She's a pain.'

One wife had three sisters and two brothers, but of these only the sister nearest in age lived within reach, and she had been the first source of comfort. 'I would have picked her to talk to anyhow, she's a lot easier to talk to than the others. We talked everything over, and she gave her opinion but said the decision was up to me.'

A woman of 37 with two sisters had found the younger one, aged 19, to be of more support than anyone else. 'She is very wise for her age and very understanding' and she was also a useful handyman and - for instance - had recently painted the front door of the house, and regularly took the 12 year old son to football matches. The older sister had been less approachable because her husband was not sympathetic towards my respondent.

One wife had five sisters and eight brothers. Her oldest sister, seven years her senior, had been marvellous. She had told her everything and had not kept anything back. Her sister told her she couldn't have two kinds of home life - husband and another man, nor should she just think about the children, since it was her own life too. Once a week she and three of her sisters met and had a good talk. Her brothers were 'down south' and she dismissed them as irrelevant.

Three wives had told their sisters before telling their parents that their marriages were ending, but none of them had said anything until the decision to separate had been taken. One said 'When I think about it, I did go to my sister, to confide in her. I was embarrassed at the length of time I was married.' She had forgotten this episode at first, since her parents had thereafter provided more continuous support. She added, 'I don't get on well with my sister when we're under the same roof, but we get on well when we're apart.' Once she had made the planned break from her husband, after only eight months of marriage, she had not again felt any need to confide in her sister. Strangely, her husband had acted in a similar manner and had turned to 'my sister mainly ... emotionally, initially, and also as a buffer in case my parents felt let down in some way.' He thought he had found it easier to talk to his sister first because of being near in age.

A bank clerkess of 31 had discussed her marriage with her sister, and with no one else, before leaving her husband, and they had continued to talk together a great deal.

The only other person to turn to a sibling before a parent had told her brother about her husband's infidelity, because her mother was temporarily abroad. She had needed someone to lean on and had found her brother and his wife to be very supportive.

A divorced sister was not necessarily seen to be an obvious choice of confidante. A wife with eight siblings, had not turned to any of them, in spite of the fact that she was so shattered by her husband's infidelity that she 'had not known what to do'. She had longed to talk to someone but had not felt close to her family. One sister had been divorced and had 'understood although her's had been entirely different'. Her younger sisters 'didn't know what was going on' and she had not discussed anything with her brothers.

A wife of 23 had also parted from an unfaithful husband and had gone to live with a sister who was about to have a divorce. She had not talked much to this sister 'because she was more involved with herself'.

A middle-aged wife had found her sister to be a great support: 'She was going through the same thing, but she's not divorced - she was thinking about it.'

Few respondents, other than those mentioned, had had frequent contact with their siblings. A wife with a pre-school age child spent a lot of time with her mother and with her sisters, who all lived in the same area, and therefore she didn't feel the need for friends.

Two husbands had valued considerate sisters. One, whose wife had suddenly left him, said 'my sister and her husband called regularly until I started to get back on my feet again ... The first three or four months were the worst.' One man had often phoned his sister, who lived some distance away: 'It was a shoulder to cry on' and he had found her far more helpful than his mother who had lived nearer but had been rather hysterical about his separation from his wife after three months of marriage.

A husband of 22 and a wife of 25 had both been upheld in rejection of their spouse by, respectively, a sister and a brother who had been quick to run down the erring spouse. The first had been described by his sister as a good catch, giving his young wife all she needed for their house within six months, while his wife had gallivanted around and 'was the talk of the street'. The other said she and her brother could talk till three in the morning, and she would 'feel great' when he told her 'your husband was never in your league'.

Practical Help

Five wives and two husbands had, at some stage, lived in a sibling's home, but by the time of divorce all had moved to their own homes except for one of the men who did not live with his married sister until immediately after the divorce, having been earlier 'staying with my pal'.

The second of these husbands had, apparently, been welcomed into the homes of most of his seven siblings 'sleeping wherever I get a bed. I'm lucky to have so many brothers and my wee sister' but his permanent base was with his parents.

The women who had been given temporary homes by siblings (three by sisters and two by brothers) had all been grateful for a sympathetic ear. One had been disappointed that her own flat was not quite ready to move into on the day that she and her husband had planned to separate, each into a newly purchased flat. Instead, she went for two months to her brother and sister-in-law, feeling let down. But she found this to be a blessing in disguise, having 'constant moral support' and not having to readjust to living on her own straightaway. 'They had three young children, which didn't give me time to brood.' And another said 'My sister was the best. She offered me a home and then helped me with househunting and jobhunting.'

Brothers barely counted when it came to looking after children. They were seen as play companions, whereas sisters took charge of children after school hours (for payment, in one case), in evenings or, once, for a holiday.

A middle-aged man had ambivalent feelings about his sister, who must have had some influence on his marriage. For ten years he had employed her to cook for him, his wife and children and to look after the children in school holidays, while his wife was at work. After his wife left him, this arrangement continued for him alone and for the children at weekends, but he described his sister as 'very nosey' and he had not told her for several months that his wife would be leaving him. His wife later told me,

> I always had his sister in the house. She all but lived
> there. That was one of the big factors. Before we were
> married and after, her whole time occupation was looking
> after her brother. My sister-in-law has done more harm to
> the kids than anyone. She was always whispering poisonous
> remarks to them. She would bring them bags of sweets and
> crisps which I didn't want them to have.

On the other hand, 'She's the kindest person I know, and my mother used to say she'd never get married and I shouldn't grudge her looking after my children.' The

pendulum swung again as she remembered that one of her children had recently told
her 'auntie hates you, Mum' and 'he told me some of the things she's said to him
over the years. He's told me if his auntie wasn't there, he'd live there. I've a
feeling he goes there every day for lunch.'

Practical help, like emotional support, was given by parents and siblings or
neither, for the most part. There was one slight exception, in that brothers who
gave practical help tended to give it instead of fathers. This was perhaps because
any practical help from fathers was often passive and in the form of housing,
where the mother played a more active part. Practical help from brothers was sometimes in the form of housing, where parents were not available. Two brothers were
singled out for mention for having been good to their siblings' children, where
there was no grandfather, and two gave some legal information from experience of
their own divorces.

Siblings Who Gave No Help

Several respondents said that their siblings were too young to be of use. Some
were still at school. Others were not yet seen to be adult: 'He was a late baby.
He's only 18. He wasn't able to cope. He wasn't interested.' Another brother who
was eager to help, was not allowed to: a wife of 22 with children of 4 and $2\frac{1}{2}$
reported that her 18 year old brother would say to her 'do you think I'm stupid?
I could look after them.'

Some siblings were thought to be preoccupied with their own difficulties. 'I never
take my troubles to any of them. They've got kids of their own; they knew what it
was like.' 'My sister is nervous and has enough troubles of her own.' 'They've got
their own problems. A marriage that goes smoothly, there's something far wrong.'
This attitude was the opposite of attitudes to people outside the family, whether
friends or professionals, where it was often said that only those who had had
similar marital difficulties would be able to understand.

A husband of 46, previously a labourer, but unemployed since he obtained custody
of his two children, kept his distance from his three sisters and two brothers,
saying that his life was none of their business. When he had been working, his
siblings never came to see him 'unless they were skint', which he had resented. He
had gratefully accepted one sister's gift of furniture which 'she did not need'
and he enjoyed playing darts when a brother took him to the pub on Fridays, but
otherwise he seldom saw his siblings although most of them lived nearby.

Conclusions

Siblings were undoubtedly appreciated, mainly in reinforcing parental support. The
absence of brothers would seldom have made much difference to respondents, who
mostly had more continuous support from the female members of their families.
Sisters might have been missed more, but mothers would usually have been available
to fill the gap. Siblings who became confidantes were normally those to whom the
respondents had always been close, whatever their marital status.

OTHER RELATIVES

Other members of their families, apart from any already mentioned, had made little
impact. One grandmother had helped 'in a very unobtrusive way. She said "if you
think this is the right thing to do, you do it and I'll support you" which surprised me very much ... We all love her dearly. The effect of the shock on her

worried me more than her reactions.' This wife had been very touched by her grandmother's support, as she had expected non-acceptance.

Otherwise, those who had confided in relatives had tended to use them as substitutes for parents or siblings who either were non-existent or were not emotionally close. A woman who had no sisters had turned to a woman cousin: 'She's a lot younger than me, but a lot older in her outlook. She tells me all her troubles and I tell her all mine.' A man who had no relatives except for a married cousin, thought a family tie to be important and he had had a good deal of support from his cousin and her family.

Two wives had not found it easy to talk to their parents. One had felt much closer to an uncle who was a very good listener, and the other had instinctively turned to an aunt and uncle to ask for a temporary home. They gave her 'food, shelter and love' for several months, but she was not able to talk to them any more than to her own parents. Whenever either the aunt or the uncle tried to get her to talk, she clenched her fists and became tense. Similarly, a secretary with a small daughter had lived for three years with a cousin but found that 'resentment built up' in an overcrowded house. Again, the family tie survived any strains. A driver aged 40 had left his wife and asked his parents for a home, although he had never got on with them. They allowed him to stay for one night only, and he then stayed with an aunt for seven months 'and she was lonely so we were good company for each other'.

Three respondents continued friendships with relations of their ex-spouses. A wife kept in touch with her husband's niece, and a man used to meet a male cousin of his wife's: 'We chat quite freely, although he balances a bit, sitting on the fence.' One wife described, in a very confidential tone, a friendship with her husband's aunt. 'There is one person who is completely on my side, who is a relative of his. She helped me immensely. If I had a problem, she helped me. After the divorce she told me a lot about him.'

SPOUSES

Attitudes of the divorced to their ex-spouses varied from those of warm friendship to those of almost venomous bitterness. Some found that, once the decision had been taken to end the marriage, any tension was lessened and a calmer relationship could develop. Some felt intensely bitter towards their ex-spouses as the result of deep personal hurt. The first category could help each other as they each adjusted to their single status.

Altogether, twelve husbands (20 per cent) and nineteen wives (32 per cent) had been helped by their ex-spouses. They were more likely to have had some kind of practical help than emotional support from each other, and the two were seldom combined. Further, wives were more likely than husbands to have found their spouses giving practical help, or to have found them positively unhelpful.

An examination of the 43 divorces where both spouses were interviewed shows some reciprocity of emotional support (in four couples, whereas in two others it was one-sided) but not of practical help (in only one couple was it reciprocal and in 13 it was one-sided).

There is little discernible pattern among those who received help from their spouses. They are nearly equally divided between pursuers and defenders and between age groups. Only 7 per cent of those whose de facto marriages had lasted for less than two years had been helped by their spouses, while there was a sharp increase in help for longer marriages.

Emotional Support

Although twelve husbands and nine wives (including both halves of six couples)
mentioned that they were still friendly with their ex-spouses, this often amounted
only to a cessation of bitterness and not to any active support. The sting had
been taken out of their relationship and they were able to relax when they met.
Six husbands and six wives seemed to have had emotional support from their spouses
during the period of separation. These included both halves of four couples (three
of them childless). In two other couples, a husband living alone and suffering
from loneliness, and a wife possibly anxious for a reconciliation (having lost her
new partner) were appreciative of support from their spouses, although neither
spouse reported reciprocal support. The remaining two to have appreciated support
from their spouses were one husband and one wife whose spouses were not interviewed.

Emotional support was most appreciated by social classes I and II (23 per cent);
for the remainder it was rare (6 per cent).

The nature of this emotional support was entirely one of friendship. 'We're very,
very friendly now and get on better when we're not living together.' 'We're more
friendly than we've ever been.' Some met on neutral ground, perhaps to have a
drink: 'We still go out together (but) we couldn't really live with each other.'

This theme of not being able to live together was repeated by others who had
gradually overcome their bitterness.

> It was a very fraught time when we were splitting up. It is
> difficult to be friendly with someone you've decided you
> don't want to live with ... A year after we separated we
> were fairly amicable ... (Now) we go out to dinner for
> Christmas or a birthday. The passage of time allowed any
> anger to die down.

'We're talking now. For over a year we never spoke. It dies down after a time,'
said another husband, while his wife described how she had 'bumped into' her
husband fifteen months after separation: 'We started talking. I was that nervous,
it was like a first date.'

Those who remained friendly but on a more lukewarm basis expressed it as 'I see
her from time to time. We mix in the same social crowds. Her attitudes have
changed over the two years. She is more friendly ... no longer bitter.'

There was some evidence of a social class difference among those who were anxious
not to meet each other. An accountant, a doctor's wife and a financial adviser's
wife had all been careful to avoid occasions where they might meet their spouses.
They used to check before going to a social function that their spouses had not
been invited. 'At first we had to be careful not to bump into each other. In the
end, except in the context of mutual friends, there was no problem.'

By contrast couples who, after separation, lived within a few minutes' walk of
each other in deprived areas seemed to have had no difficulty in avoiding each
other, even though they might have met in the street, in a shop or at a bus stop.
They did not seem to be worried by the possibility of a chance meeting, and they
did not lead the kind of social lives that might bring them together. Two couples
worked for the same employer: the social class II couple took steps to see that
their paths did not cross; the IIIM couple left it to chance and never happened to
meet at work.

Practical Help

It has already been noted that wives were twice as likely as husbands to have had practical help from their spouses. The likelihood of having had some practical help from a spouse increased with the de facto length of marriage.

Most practical help had been concerned with co-operation in the care of children or had been financial.

Of the 75 respondents with children, 16 (21 per cent) described practical help from their spouses. Those with custody were three times more likely than those without custody to have had this help, which was more often financial than concerned with the care of children.

In two families, a teenage boy had chosen temporarily to leave one parent (in one case a mother, in the other a father) in order to live with the other. In two other families the spouse who had left home gave substantial support in looking after the children they had left. A father of three children valued almost daily visits from his wife to their family: his wife was not interviewed. A mother of two teenage sons said, 'When it comes to the boys, I'd always send for my husband.' In particular, she had needed her husband's assistance in dealing with one son's truancy. She knew that her husband liked to be called on, and she traded on his desire to help with the boys. 'If I move, he's going to help me move. He's got the car and he takes me round the housing schemes. I've told him I'm using him for my own ends.'

While only a few expressed appreciation of help in sharing the care of their children, a few others had found their spouses positively unhelpful in their lack of concern for their children. A 42 year old father had custody of his six year old son because, he said, his wife found 'it interfered with her social life' to have the boy. A mother aged 37 was bitter that her husband no longer wanted to see their two teenage children.

Couples who agreed to share the expenses of a divorce (either equally or one third by the wife) were all childless except for one. In every case, both were earning and had thought it fair that each should contribute to the cost of the divorce, whether or not they had decided on a divorce before they had separated. Some of these couples had never met each other after separation, but had been grateful for the other's co-operation in financial matters which had then facilitated a divorce. Those who had jointly owned their homes shared the value on divorce, even if one still lived in the house and had bought the other's share.

Several wives had regularly received financial support for their children through-out the period of separation, and had had the same sum written into the divorce agreement. It had perhaps not occurred to them that inflation had reduced the value of these weekly payments. Some had also had gifts of money for specific purchases whenever they asked. However, the important point was that these wives were confident that they could rely on their husbands to continue regular payments, which had usually been made in person. This financial assistance had sometimes been linked with access to children. Husbands would bring their weekly payment and see, or take out, their children at the same time. The disadvantage of this arrangement was that it could be seen as a quid pro quo, and the father might appear to be paying to see his children. If payment ceased, so did his contact with children. 'If he doesn't come here and I don't get the maintenance, to me that's fair.' Or, 'I can stop him coming here if he doesn't pay.'

Division of possessions in the matrimonial home had not been as easy as sharing a capital sum but, once accomplished, there had sometimes been gratitude to a spouse.

One wife had not seen her husband since they separated two and a half years before
divorce and had been agreeably surprised by a gesture from him:

> It sounds very hard and unfeeling, but I missed my house
> more than my husband. I had worked hard all my married life.
> I had a nice house, a lovely house. I missed the material
> things because I'd worked for them and paid for 50 per cent
> of them. Before he sold the house, I didn't know what was
> happening. Then he got in touch with me and said to take what
> I wanted.

Another wife had told her husband that it was 'hardly fair' that he had both the
house and the furniture, so he gave her £200 which satisfied her. Her husband told
me that this was 'a mouth to mouth agreement. I said I'd pay for the divorce if
she didn't ask for half the value of the flat.'

Some husbands had given help in very practical ways such as advice over car
maintenance, or repairing a vacuum cleaner (this, where a new male partner was not
adept at repairs!). Transfer of house tenancies had been seen by some as helpful,
and by others as automatic. The difference was that some husbands had made an offer
to vacate the matrimonial home. Others had waited to be told by solicitors or the
housing department that a wife with children was entitled to the home, or that a
husband was liable to pay the rent until he transferred the tenancy to his wife.

Unhelpful Spouses

Spite had entered a few marital relationships. One wife (whose husband could not
be traced for interview) reported a series of petty incidents on both sides after
they had separated. They seemed to have taken a pleasure in scoring against each
other.

Five wives and two husbands described how their spouses had removed furniture from
the marital home without consultation. For instance, one wife returned, with her
children, to the matrimonial home after a transfer of tenancy, to find that her
husband had 'taken the carpets, my suite, my dishes, even the toilet roll holder
off the wall; he left the cooker for the simple reason it wasn't working.'

Other examples of spouses being obstructive or hurtful included acrimonious
discussions over the division of property. 'Then we had to split the possessions
which was not very easy ... We did it after a few not very nice phone calls. We
didn't meet.' Four husbands told me that they were prevented by court interdict
from visiting their wives' homes, and these reports were borne out by the three
wives who were interviewed.

Five couples had lived separate lives under one roof until one spouse could find
alternative accommodation. Some had provided services for the other; some had not.
'If I was in when he was, I made his meals and did his washing. Rather than make
it worse, I'd rather be busy.' All had found the arrangement stressful: 'I ended
up going out every night. If two people are living separately in the same house
and hating each other, there's not much else you can do.'

Bitterness and anger against their spouses were shown at interview by three
husbands and three wives, for all of whom the sense of rejection had been a severe
personal blow, half of them having spouses who had found new partners.

> If you adore somebody and have no inkling ... to contrive
> to hurt and not have the strength of character to discuss

> things ... she was incredibly clinical, which was all the
> more hurtful ... It seems incredible that you can be madly
> in love with somebody even through three months of hell.
> Then you can just switch it off like switching off a light
> switch.

Others had suffered shock when their spouses had left them, apparently without
warning. With hindsight, they had realised that the action was not entirely unexpected.

> It was like somebody hitting me with a sledgehammer. I
> should have expected it because she gave plenty of warning,
> asking me to pack in the job I was in, which I did agree
> with her (where he had had easy access to alcohol).

By the time of divorce, the initial shock had usually worn off and respondents had
become resigned to their fate.

A number of both husbands and wives insisted that they would never remarry 'and
risk everything again'. The hurt was too recent for them to contemplate another
marriage. 'I'd rather live with someone, to be honest.' And 'I can't imagine myself ever wanting to get married again. I shouldn't have got married the first
time around. I should have thought about it more. I want my independence and
privacy too much.'

Because of unheeded warnings, it might have been difficult to ascertain how many
marriages had come to an abrupt end and how many had gradually died. The question
was, in any case, not asked since it was peripheral to the study, but in any
future research this might be a useful variable to investigate. In eleven divorces
(14 per cent of the total) respondents reported, without being asked, that there
had been previous separations. Possibly others had had the same experience.

The difficulty of deciding whether to continue with the marriage or to separate was
described by one wife:

> If your marriage is driving you up the wall, you're in a
> terrible dilemma. It's a very frustrating position, to be
> where you don't want to be, and you've nowhere else to go,
> and you can't see the light at the end of the tunnel. It
> never gets better. It must get worse. You're both trapped.

Another wife had had no such doubts and compared herself with her sister, whose
husband was unemployed and neglectful of his family.

> My sister thought I was crackers, stark raving mad. I had a
> husband who gave me security and who came home at the same
> time every night, but I didn't have love, and she did.

The loneliness after a marriage had ended was often hard to bear. After 17 years
of marriage, one woman had found that 'the loneliness is terrible when your husband
has left. You've no longer got someone to share things with. It's a worse shock if
you've had a happy marriage.' Another wife said there was not even someone to
discuss a television programme with, and a man who was living in digs at divorce,
asked what was the use of being divorced when you're 56? 'You want your family
then. She had the best years of my life and threw them back in my face.'

A Complete Break

Respondents were not asked about frequency of contact with their spouses during
the separation. While this would have been a useful question, it might have been
difficult to quantify the replies. They were, of course, asked whether their
spouses had been helpful since separation, and in giving information about this,
it was apparent that at least 24 couples (31 per cent) had not met since separation.
For them there had been a complete break from living together to separating and
never making any attempt to meet again. Some had agreed, before separation, that
they would get divorced while others had had no discussion: in those cases,
either one partner started divorce proceedings without direct consultation, or the
couple spoke to each other by telephone.

Half of the childless couples did not meet after separation, but also nine couples
with children had made a complete break (in one case, the father was in prison,
but the wife had not visited him and hoped never to see him again). As might be
expected, there was a significant difference in behaviour between those with and
those without children: 39 of the 48 couples with children had met after separation, but only 14 of the 29 childless couples had done so.

Children in a few of the families where their parents did not meet again had
occasionally seen the absent parent, but four of these fathers had not seen their
children since the separation (one being in prison) while two other such fathers
and one mother had eventually lost touch.

Half of those divorced by the age of 25 had not seen their spouses since separating. Proportions of other age groups were lower, varying from 39 per cent (for
wives aged 31-35) to 20 per cent (wives aged over 35).

The grounds for divorce made no difference to whether or not couples met again.
Roughly one third of couples divorcing for adultery, for unreasonable behaviour or
for separation did not meet. For periods of separation to divorce lasting for more
than one year, the shorter separations were more likely not to have met, except
that couples separated for one year or less were the most likely to have met.

Social class appeared to have no affect on the incidence of meetings after separation.

The factor which was the greatest determinant in influencing couples' meeting
appeared to be the de facto length of marriage. In 78 per cent of the 18 marriages
which had lasted for two years or less, the couples did not meet again after
separating. They included every one of the seven marriages (9 per cent of the total
of 77) which lasted for 16 months or less. It was not that these couples had
married on short acquaintance. One, married at 18, had known her husband since she
was 12; one, married at 19, had gone out with her husband for five years before
marriage. Nor were they all teenage brides: the mean age of these seven brides had
been 21. One said 'We'd gone out together long enough, but we just didn't know
each other.'

Perceptions of Marriage

Some respondents had known of faults in their partners but had hoped that marriage
would change them. A nurse had married at 22 partly because she had liked her
husband's family very much. Although 'I had grave misgivings before the marriage,
I thought I could change him.' Another husband 'was on drugs when I met him,
sleeping pills and so on, and I used to suggest that he cut down'. Several said
that it was too easy to get married, but they seldom had ideas for a remedy,

although a few suggested that marriage should cost more. There was one mention of the need for positive preparation for marriage. This came from a man of 31, who had learned from a Catholic friend that priests have several sessions with couples before marriage.

Two wives gave such lucid ideas about marriage that it seems worth quoting them. One was a girl of 22, married at 19 for only three months:

> I think nowadays divorce is getting so common. You get
> married and you're in love, and you think it'll be just
> like staying at home. Every young girl wants to get married.
> If someone asks you, you say yes. You don't want to be left
> on the shelf. I think we were too young mentally. You can
> fool yourself you're in love ... He was the only boy I'd
> ever went steady with. He was the first thing to come into
> my mind in the morning, and the last thing at night ...
> Parents should have more say in whether their children
> should get married. They know you better than you know
> yourself. If they made a law that you couldn't get married
> without your parents' consent, that would be a help. If you
> really loved each other, you could wait.

Of her group of six friends at school, all had married, but only one was still married, now that they were all 22. She would NEVER get married again.

> I might live with them. My Mum says you might then get
> married, but I don't see what that piece of paper does.
> Marriage doesn't mean anything any more ... The way things
> are going now, every person is going to get married six or
> seven times. If you live together you don't need to see a
> lawyer and drag it out and get more hurt.

The other wife, in a managerial post, had given some thought to the disadvantages of marriage:

> How fundamental is the belief that there should be a major
> relationship in one's life? I find it hard to be autonomous ...
> I'm not sure a one to one relationship is ideal. I still
> wonder about it. Really I feel it's that Scotland is still
> tied to a one to one relationship. Most Scottish men have a
> problem dealing with women. Very few Scottish men like
> women. They like a traditional relationship, with a passive
> wife in the home, while they subscribe to the rhetoric.

She summed it up as 'the problem of single women in a culture that is geared to marriage'. She was reluctant to risk another partnership, let alone another marriage.

Conclusions

Although about one quarter of the respondents had had some help from their spouses, few had had any real or continuing support. By the time of divorce most had come to accept the inevitability of a legal termination of the marriage and had lost any bitterness that they had felt on separating, even though one third of the couples had never met since they had separated.

NEW PARTNERS

Six respondents (5 per cent), one man and five women, had moved straight from the
marital home to live with a new partner. They were still living with their new
partners at the time of divorce. Meanwhile, a further 25 (21 per cent), nineteen
men and six women, had started cohabiting with a new partner, and a further seven
(6 per cent), three men and four women had a new partner whom they seemed likely
to marry. Therefore 38 in all (32 per cent), 23 men and 15 women, had a new
partner by the time of divorce. Two (one man and one woman) had already remarried
(legally permissible three weeks after divorce); four men and three women had made
arrangements to remarry shortly while others intended to do so but had no specific
plans. These figures give some support to the findings of Dunnell (1979) that
cohabitation is more usual for the divorced and separated than for the single, and
that 30 per cent of second marriages start as cohabitations.

Remarriage could bring problems. A man of 22 was planning to remarry and was
buying a house with his new girlfriend, who knew about his first marriage and
about the son whom he no longer saw. His problem was that he could not bring himself to tell her parents that he was divorced, although he had known them for over
a year and liked them very much. He showed some perception of their feelings when
he said to me, 'I don't know how you'd feel yourself if your daughter had a boy-
friend who'd been married before.' His fears were echoed in the experience of
another man who was planning his second marriage, but 'Once her parents found out
I was married, they wanted her to have nothing to do with me, so I told them I
was divorced ages ago and they were all right.'

New partners had been helpful during separation in 82 per cent of cases where they
were established and emotionally supportive in 79 per cent. Some respondents could
not put this support into words, but others were able to express it: 'My girlfriend's the only one I'd ever sit and talk to.' 'The man I'm living with now, he
helped me more than anybody.' On the whole, support seemed self-evident. Several
had given reciprocal support to each other, where both had had a broken marriage.

Those few who claimed to have had no particular support from their new partner
said, for instance, 'I'd got over it all by the time I met her' or 'I don't like
discussing my husband with anyone.' One couple had both quickly formed new
relationships and had not felt the need of support from their new partners, after
a marriage that had gradually died. Some acknowledged practical help in the form
of housing.

Eleven of the twelve defenders who were divorced for adultery were living with the
same third parties at the time of divorce. The twelfth was a wife whose new
partner had subsequently left her to return to his own wife. Six defenders had not
been divorced for adultery although they were living with a new partner. Four of
them (three wives and one husband) had given their consent to divorce after two
years separation, while two husbands had been divorced for unreasonable behaviour.

Help from new partners had often been unimportant or irrelevant because they had
not been known during the marriage.

CHILDREN

Among those interviewed, 76 (63 per cent) had children of the marriage, including
some aged 16 or over and outside the jurisdiction of the court. This represented
49 divorces (64 per cent of the total of 77), 48 having children under 16. A few
respondents had consciously sought help or support from their children, whether
toddler, school age or adult, but many more admitted to some appreciation of their

presence. Any such support would have been continuously available to respondents with custody of their children and the cumulative effect could have been considerable. Taking together those who had actively leaned on their children and those who had been consciously glad of their company, 32 (42 per cent of respondents with children), an equal number of husbands and of wives, had had some support from their children; this included parents with and without custody. Husbands who had custody of children under 16 were significantly more likely than wives with custody to have had emotional support from their children.

During interviews, husbands who had the custody of their children gave the impression of being conscious of their unusual responsibilities. Therefore, support may well have been reciprocal in these cases, with children appreciating the conscientious care of their fathers. Two of the ten husbands who had custody of children were unemployed and were particularly vulnerable to loneliness. They did not have the same social contacts open to them as did mothers at home with children. It might have aroused suspicion if they had wanted to drop in for cups of tea with mothers in the same predicament. This threw them back on any resources available within their families of origin or on the company of their own children. More wives than husbands with custody were unemployed: 11 (35 per cent) out of 31, while some others worked part time only.

The proportion of children described as supportive steadily declined through social classes I to IV from 100 per cent (admittedly only one respondent) to 27 per cent, but rose to 64 per cent for class V. No other factors distinguished those parents who had received support from their children from those who had not.

Emotional Support

Unlike other donors of support, children were not necessarily conscious of helping their parents. They may even have been too young to understand what was happening. A wife who was deserted by her husband when their only child was three months old, said of the baby 'He was the only thing that kept me going. It's surprising what you can do if someone is dependent on you.' A mother of four children (aged 10 to 4 at separation) said, 'You get very lonely, especially when the kids are in their bed. You talk to your children like as though they're adults. You keep the kids up to talk to them at night.' Other parents described their children as 'a comfort' or 'very good company'.

Practical Help

While some parents reported that their children had been helpful by doing the ironing or some cooking, it is possible that these tasks would have been undertaken whether or not the parents had been separated. No parents described any practical help that seemed particularly related to the absence of the other parent. Indeed, some single parents were fiercely proud of being able to manage without calling on their children to help them. Two women whose sons were in employment received financial contributions which covered the cost of food but no more, both women possibly seeking to compensate their sons for the lack of a father by allowing them as much spending money as possible from their wages.

Problems Arising from Separation and Divorce

It was no part of this research to investigate the effect of parental separation and divorce on children. But inevitably some information was gathered on this subject and should be reported in the context of a sample of divorced respondents.

In twelve of the 48 divorces in which there were children under 16, one parent
showed no interest in the children and did not see them. Among parents who did not
have custody, seven fathers and one mother interviewed had seldom, if ever, seen
their children since their marriages had broken down. Five of their spouses (four
mothers and the one father) were interviewed and confirmed this. A further four
wives who had custody of their children and whose husbands were not interviewed,
reported a similar lack of contact between children and fathers.

The children who did not see one parent tended to be very young. Most had been
under two years old when their parents had separated. In most cases, the absent
parents did not show even a token interest in their children at the interview.
Sometimes they seemed to rationalise, but they did not try to make excuses for not
seeing their families. Fathers baldly said, 'It's better to forget about it' or
'He doesn't really know me. I feel it's better if he doesn't see me.' The mothers
of these children appeared unconcerned, even relieved by this attitude: 'The
youngest was too young and the oldest one never got any attention anyway' or 'They
were glad to see the back of him.' The only mother who showed little interest in
her children was aged 20 at the time of divorce and had seldom made any attempt to
see her children, now aged four and two, during the previous year. She claimed
that her husband did not allow her to see the children: 'I suppose I could go back
to the lawyer, but it's too much trouble.' Her husband said that she had not
exercised the fortnightly access granted at divorce and that she had taken the
children out only twice in the previous year.

In two families of slightly older children, the father had shown a declining
interest in them. Both fathers had lost touch with their children (aged 8 and 6,
and 12 and 10) before divorce. One mother was relieved that the father, living a
mile away, had made little attempt to see his children. The other mother said one
of her children was very bitter about his father's neglect.

Parents with custody of their children preferred any access by the other parent to
be regular and predictable, and frequent enough for a child to understand and
anticipate.

> He used to turn up every second weekend and take the
> children down for the weekend. Then he started showing up
> every two months, and just as the kids were settling down
> here, he'd come and take them down there ... But he
> disappeared before I got it sorted out.

'If it is only now and again, I wish he wouldn't come,' said another mother.

There was no evidence of children being spoiled during access by the missing
parent: no parent complained that a child was receiving gifts or treats which
could not be afforded at home. Rather was the opposite true: some mothers were
aggrieved that their ex-husbands did not buy clothes for their children when they
took them out for the day. Promises, perhaps made to keep a child's affection and
then broken, could be upsetting. A father of four children had told his eight year
old son that the boy could live with him. Failure to follow up this offer was seen
by the mother as leading to behaviour problems for the boy.

In six of the 27 families where both parents were interviewed, the two parents
gave conflicting accounts of access. Five fathers claimed that they saw their
children frequently, while the mothers reported reluctance on the part of their
children to visit their fathers. 'If they see him in the street, they never speak
to him. They cross the road. And he never comes near to see them.' The children of
the sixth family lived with their father who said:

I was going to let her have them once a week, but she
didn't want that. She's not been (to fetch them) for four
or five months now ... It annoys me her never coming to see
them. They used to say 'do you think she'll come today?'
They don't bother now.

Meanwhile, the mother told me 'the two girls come up without their Dad's consent.
If he ever finds out, he'll take it out on them.' One of the girls was with the
mother when I arrived to interview her, but left shortly after my arrival.

The problem of access must always be a vexed one. The relationship between a child
and a parent with access could perhaps be compared with that of a couple before
their marriage. In both cases, meetings are apt to be on someone else's territory,
rather than in a shared home. While it is often thought that a child should keep
in touch with both parents, Goldstein, Freud and Solnit (1973) wrote that,
'Children have difficulty in relating positively to, profiting from, and maintaining the contact with two psychological parents who are not in positive contact
with each other.' The authors recommended that the non-custodial parent should
have no legal right to visit the child, and that the custodial parent, rather than
the court, should decide whether or not the other parent should have access.

Many parents said that their children had been unaffected by the marriage breakdown; they usually also showed a lack of interest in their children's progress at
school.

No parent interviewed seemed to have any conception of the caring role of a health
visitor, who was seen as a giver of inoculations or as someone who called to check
on the children's health, and a suggestion that the health visitor might have been
helpful could be resented. 'She was always satisfied' seemed to imply an inspect-
orial function.

It seemed to be rare for parents to have met a teacher, let alone to have explained to the school that events at home might influence school work. They mostly
assumed, when questioned, that teachers knew about the marital separation, but
without knowing who would have given the information. Two parents even regretted
having told teachers about their separations: 'I wish I hadn't told the teacher.
She's continually looking for emotional upsets ... She's quite young and over-
concerned.'

Fourteen parents (including two couples) mentioned teachers when talking about
their children. Seven (including one couple) had found teachers sympathetic and
helpful, especially with teenage children. Only one (a mother) realised that her
15 year old daughter, who was 'really upset, and was embarrassed about it all'
had 'needed someone outside to talk to'. Mother and daughter had both appreciated
the concern of the teacher who had befriended the girl.

Parents of teenagers in four families had been conscious that marital breakdown
had led to truancy, but they had taken no action until summoned to a hearing at
the school. Some parents seemed willing to collude with the truants ('they weren't
getting learned anything') and had been mildly grateful to teachers for a
sympathetic attitude after the parental separation had been explained. Two fathers
(both with custody) considered that the truanting was no concern of their's.
'You're not on trial: It's your children who are' and (indignantly) 'they was
punishing me instead of my daughter.'

Two parents of primary school boys considered that teachers should know that their
children's changed behaviour (one was 'boisterous' and one was 'aye crying') might
have been caused by parental separation. There had been no subsequent discussion

with teachers.

A father of four children had requested and received permission from the head
teacher to have each of his children in turn for a week, bringing school work with
them. The mother, who had custody, also reported this, and added that the youngest
child was to have a week's holiday with his own teacher, whom she had found most
helpful.

Two mothers had not told teachers about their separations until they had been
forced into it - one because, at a parents' meeting, teachers reported disappointment in a teenage boy's work, and the other because the school asked why the
father had not signed some form for his seven year old daughter. Parents who had
spoken to one teacher about one child's problems had never told the teachers of
their other children about the marital separation. They 'supposed' it was known,
as did parents who did not communicate with any teacher.

On the whole, children's behaviour at school was of little concern to parents who,
in turn, did not think that home circumstances were of any concern of teachers.
Few of these separated parents ever went to parents' meetings. One father who did
go, said he was the only father present among thirty mothers and he felt disapproval from the headmistress who talked about his 'problem'.

At least six mothers and one father had been conscious that their children had
reacted badly to the marriage breakdown, especially if they had hidden the true
state of affairs from their children. One father with custody of two children,
considering the alternatives open to him, said of the effect on his children: 'It
had to be adverse. But had my wife and I not separated, it would have been more
adverse.'

I got the impression that parents tended to ascribe to their children their own
feelings of relief, irritation or bitterness, without having observed what was
happening, or else not wanting to think that their children might have suffered.
Parents were understandably pre-occupied with their own emotions.

Most of the few reports of changes in children's behaviour were of teenagers whose
parents had tried to keep from them any indication that there were marriage
problems. Separation, anticipated by parents, came as a shock to these teenagers.
'It was pretty shattering for them, coming out of the blue ... I suppose it was a
real tragedy for them. They didn't know what was going on. They didn't realise it
had got to that stage. There'd been no wild arguments.' Or 'We kept it from them ...
(He) thought the world of his Dad. He's feeling neglected now.'

Explanations to Children

Some parents recounted difficulties in telling their children about the marriage
breakdown and the reason for the departure of one parent, although I did not
question them about this. A few pretended that fathers were working away from home
or that they were in the army. Awkward questions such as 'why does that man take
out my mother when she is your wife?' were dodged. Possibly a fear of losing a
father was expressed as 'will my Dad still be my Dad when you're divorced?' The
mother of a teenage boy, who didn't like her sharing a bed with a man he had met
only once before going to live in his house, explained to her son that she and her
husband had had no sexual life for many years, in spite of sharing a bed. Some
parents preferred to keep their children in ignorance. 'They don't know about the
divorce. They still cling on to the hope that one day their Daddy'll come back.
They haven't seen him for six months but they still talk about him.' One man,
separated for 16 years (and therefore ineligible for inclusion in the sample) had

never told his ten year old daughter that he was not married to her mother.

About half of the prisoners' wives in Morris's study had not explained to their children that the father was in prison (Morris, 1965). It seemed likely that some of these children were less ignorant of the situation than their mothers thought, especially as a number of them were taken to visit fathers in prison. Marris found, in some of the widows in his sample, a similar reluctance or inability to tell children the cause of the father's absence (Marris, 1958).

Change of Home

Four families of children (8 per cent of those with children under 16) moved, with one parent, to the home of grandparents and later returned to the original family home. In ten other families (21 per cent), children had alternated between both parents, eventually living with five fathers and five mothers. In three of these families, a child was apparently being used in order to give one parent some priority with the housing department. A ten year old boy shared a room and kitchen with his father and the latter's new partner: both parents told me that the father would thus qualify for a local authority house. In some of these ten families it seemed that the parents had given more consideration to their own needs than to the children's welfare: physical possession of children could be a useful bargaining weapon in divorce proceedings, one parent agreeing to access if the other paid aliment.

In each of three of these ten families, two children had spent some time with foster parents: all of them had had several changes of home and in all three families the father eventually had custody. The court had not asked for a report of the welfare of any of these children before granting divorce, but two of the three families had been before Children's Hearings which had referred them to a Sheriff for a decision to grant interim custody to the fathers. Two of the three mothers were probably medically unfit to continue keeping their children: the fathers had had no immediate homes to offer, and the children were placed in foster homes for one year and for five months respectively, before going to live with their fathers. A third pair of children, aged a few months and two years when their mother had left home, had had five changes of residence in the following eighteen months. They went successively to maternal grandparents, to a foster home, to hospital (with dysentery), to paternal grandparents and finally to their father's new home with his prospective stepmother. A month after the divorce, the social work supervision order by the Children's Hearing came to an end. The paternal grandmother had been the only witness at the divorce, when custody had been given to the father.

Information about Children's Welfare at Divorce

The court is meant to obtain evidence about the welfare of the children before a divorce is granted. Divorce may not be granted '... unless and until the court is satisfied ... that arrangements have been made for the care and upbringing of the child and that those arrangements are satisfactory or are the best which can be devised in the circumstances' (Matrimonial Proceedings (Children) Act, 1958, s.8).

When divorces were heard in open court (as three quarters of this sample were), written information about the children tended to consist of a brief statement in the summons such as 'It is in the best interest of the said children that they should be in the custody of the pursuer. They are in her care and are happy and well looked after' (Eekelaar and Clive, 1977). The pursuer was sometimes the only witness in court to the children's welfare, whether or not they were in the pursuer's care. Oral evidence was often cursory, perhaps relating to the number of bedrooms in the family house, and a statement that the children were happy (but presumably no pursuer hoping for a divorce would be likely to say anything else).

Since the advent of affidavit evidence, an 'independent' witness has been required to testify to the children's well-being. This witness may be the mother of the pursuer and she presumably is likely to be biased and, if the children are in the care of the defender, not to know much about their welfare.

In virtually every divorce in this sample where there were children, the court can have had almost no information about their welfare before coming to decisions about custody or access. There was little sign of any attempt by the court to identify any children who may have been distressed about custody or access provision. In only one of the 77 divorces investigated had there been a social welfare report about a child, and that was ordered by the court because a mother had refused to allow her husband access to her son whom he had not tried to see for three years. According to the mother, her husband had asked for access only in order to give her extra expense (in paying for a report), and he had sub-sequently withdrawn his request. This report had been prepared by a social worker, although it is more usual in Scotland for judges to ask advocates to undertake such investigations. Social workers are paid a fixed fee of about £10 for compiling a child welfare report, whereas an advocate, being self-employed, is paid a much higher fee for the time spent, as well as travelling and other expenses. The cost to anyone who is not legally aided could be considerable.

Conclusions

In 1977, there were children of the marriage in about 6000 divorce actions in Scotland (calculated from Civil Judicial Statistics, Scotland, 1977). Probably well over 10,000 children had parents who were divorced that year.

Little seems to be known of children's perceptions and experiences of parental separation and divorce. Risks of delinquency were twice as high among the children of divorced or separated parents as among all children in Douglas's national sample of children (Douglas, Ross and Simpson, 1968). Murchison provided evidence for the Finer Committee, partly based on statistical information from Douglas, that children of divorced or separated parents have a consistently lower educa-tional attainment than other children (Murchison, 1974). Not enough is known about the effect of divorce on children. It might be illuminating to follow up children of divorced parents to find out what their experiences had been: how much they had understood, what had been their feelings about and contact with the absent parent, what explanation had been given to them, and whether there had been attributable after-effects. Nearly half of the respondents with children had been aware of some emotional support from their children. The children themselves may have received reciprocal support, but probably some of them felt bewildered or rejected. Particularly vulnerable were the children who had several changes of home and those who were not told that the absent parent would not return to live with them.

Parents had had little appreciation of services for their children or of the need for such services. It would probably have been illuminating to have interviewed health visitors, teachers and others who had been in touch with the children in this research.

CHAPTER 8

FRIENDS, NEIGHBOURS AND COLLEAGUES

It was not easy to distinguish between friends, neighbours and colleagues since
the terms could be interchangeable. Others, too, have found it difficult to
differentiate between 'friends' and 'neighbours' (e.g. Morris, 1965). At first,
Townsend's respondents claimed to have nothing to do with their neighbours, but
he later found that 'neighbour' was taken to exclude relatives and friends
(Townsend, 1957).

Interviews were only semi-structured, and respondents could have mentioned in any
order these three categories of informal contacts, any or none of which might have
included another. No conclusions can therefore be drawn about the number of respondents who claimed to have had help from one, rather than another, of these
three categories. Any analysis must look at all three simultaneously.

In all, 49 (41 per cent) said that they had been helped by friends, 44 (37 per
cent) by colleagues and 30 (25 per cent) by neighbours. Four people (three
husbands and one wife) described helpful friends, neighbours and colleagues, all
separately. Thirty described a combination of two of these and fifty one
described only one (23 friends, 10 neighbours and 18 colleagues). 'Colleagues' has
been used as an umbrella term to cover anyone at a place of work, including
employers.

Emotional Support

Those who had had emotional support from friends, neighbours or colleagues were
50 per cent of all husbands and 60 per cent of all wives. They were fairly evenly
spread throughout the age range of the sample, but their numbers steadily
decreased the lower the social class. Patterns were very similar for friends, for
neighbours or for colleagues separately.

In her study of young women with small children, Gavron found that 'relationships
with friends and neighbours were far more common among the middle-class than
working-class wives.' None of her middle-class respondents had had no friends, but
25 per cent of her 48 working-class respondents claimed to be without friends,
while 69 per cent of the middle-class had contacts with neighbours, but only 29
per cent of the working-class (Gavron, 1966).

There was a preponderence of the childless who had been emotionally supported by friends, neighbours or colleagues. For instance, 56 per cent of those with no children under 16 described emotional support from friends, compared with 23 per cent of those with children. These figures could be partly explained by the fact that many of the childless were in social classes I and II and were living alone in owner-occupied homes at divorce.

The untrained but receptive ear of a sympathetic friend, neighbour or colleague was an important source of support for 66 (55 per cent). Few put their indebtedness into words in the way that they had done for their parents, but the description 'sympathetic' was frequently used. It seemed that what was most appreciated here was a ready listener who did not ask questions, and who sympathised and agreed with what was said, thereby bolstering up morale at a time when the drawbacks of separation were becoming apparent. Some wanted to be reassured that they had done the right thing. 'They were mixed around here; some were very sympathetic and saw my side, but a few didn't.' 'When you first split up, you feel really down. My friend said my children were wearing dirty clothes for the first time in their lives, but my pal was good. If you can talk to someone it makes you feel better. Just to talk, it was a help.'

Men needed this outlet as well as women: 32 per cent of husbands interviewed and 38 per cent of wives had had emotionally supportive friends. Of those in employment, 24 per cent of husbands and 42 per cent of wives had had supportive colleagues. Fewer neighbours gave emotional support (to 10 per cent of husbands and to 13 per cent of wives). One husband said '... the bloke I work with. You've got to have someone to talk to. I thought it was very good to have someone to talk to who didn't ask questions, but just listened,' and another husband had leaned heavily on an old school friend for the first six months after separation, when he had 'emotional difficulties. It was a difficult time, an awfully uncertain time after we'd made the decision.'

The need to talk was often a continuing one, and many listeners must have had their patience stretched. 'All my friends have helped by sitting listening. I went on and on about it at first.' 'I talked it out of my system to all my friends.' Listeners were not always face to face. Some lived hundreds of miles away and gave support in long telephone conversations or in letters.

It was considered by several that a friend who had also experienced marital breakdown was likely to be particularly sympathetic and understanding even when 'her's was different'. 'People who have been through it themselves are aware of how you feel.' A young wife thought she had been lucky in being able to turn to two girlfriends who had been divorced and a third who was going through the process of being divorced. Another wife had been surprised to find, when she talked about her own marriage, that many of her friends had unhappy marriages also: 'When you find you're not abnormal and there's thousands of you going about, you stop feeling sorry for yourself.' A clerkess was able to turn her unhappy experience to good use when she talked to a friend who worked beside her. 'I tell her all my problems and she tells me all her problems. That way, you get all your advice back again. I just tell her what to do if her man comes in drunk. I've been through it.' It was a comfort to find others in the same predicament and to have companionship in adversity.

Exchanging confidences could change a relationship. One husband had had more support from one professional colleague than from anyone else. 'We spent a lot of time together. We had been friends and colleagues for a long time. It changed the basis of the friendship. When I began to talk to him, he began to talk about his problems too.'

There was a general consensus that a more genuine understanding came from someone

who had also had an unhappy marriage. It was seen as a necessary qualification in
a listener by a husband who had been a little disappointed by the friend he knew
best. 'He knew us both, and knew how I felt, but he hadn't had much experience of
life's problems.' A lorry driver was less convinced that divorced friends could
help. His friends were 'mostly divorced; sometimes they're sitting there and
moaning to you.'

When a couple split up, their previously shared friends were faced with divided
loyalties. They could choose between taking the side of one partner and ignoring
the other, trying to bridge the gap between both or ceasing to see either. The
first was the obvious choice if the friendship had started through a common
interest with one partner, such as work or a hobby. If the friendship had been a
foursome between two male colleagues and their wives, then the separated wife was
likely to lose touch. One wife said 'I'd lost touch with so many old friends.
Friends we had made were all married couples. All the friends I had were my
husband's football friends and their wives. Our social life was around them.'
Another said that there 'was no animosity' from her husband's colleagues, who had
been joint friends, 'but I would have felt a bit disloyal seeing them'. A woman
whose marriage had lasted for fourteen years was sad that she no longer saw her
closest friend, whose husband 'was an old chum of my husband's. They were awfully
good when I came up here.' Then they suddenly dropped her and she ascribed this to
the fact that they were still seeing her husband. 'I used to hear tittle-tattle
about my ex,' and she passed it on to her friend, who would look embarrassed and
say that she knew that already. A doctor had also lost a friend who 'had been a
student friend of mine and was one of my closest friends, but he sided with my
wife'.

The other side of this coin was shown by those who had kept their shared friends,
to the exclusion of their spouse. 'Most of the couples we used to go about with
had me to their houses and were most helpful. They didn't take sides with him at
all.' (In that case, the husband was possibly being censured by joint friends for
leaving his wife for the wife of another friend).

A husband whose wife worked in the same hospital found that anything he said might
be passed back to his wife. 'It was a very difficult situation. People tended to
take sides and I was getting uptight. It was not paranoia, it just happened.' He
solved his difficulty by leaving the hospital.

Ambivalence led to awkwardness for one couple who had each, in turn, left the
matrimonial house in favour of the other. The wife commented that 'my friend who
lives nextdoor was friends with us both. I haven't discussed it much with her. She
probably thinks I should have stayed with my husband. I was more friends with the
girl and my husband with hers, so it was bound to be awkward.' Her husband said of
the other husband 'he didn't take sides. He'd blame me for the marriage break-up
and then he'd blame my wife.'

A temporary withdrawal of friendship was experienced by several, particularly by
professional people, just when they most needed friends. One wife had understood
the difficulties faced by shared friends: 'Some people who had been mutual friends
ended by taking sides, not because of the rights and wrongs, but because it put a
tremendous strain on them ... Two people in particular who tended to drop me have
recently become friendly again.' Meanwhile, her husband had found friends to be
embarrassed: 'The reactions of mutual friends, they don't know which side to take.
I lost some friends and so did she.' Another husband 'had to accept that I lost
touch with people for a while, because they were in the middle. Friends were torn
between two stools.' Another professional man reported 'some relationships with
mutual friends have been quite upsetting. Only one pair stayed on a good relationship with us both. Another couple don't want anything to do with me now.' A wife

who had deserted her husband and four children had thereby lost a number of
friends among her ex-neighbours. She thought that some would welcome her back
(although this might have been wishful thinking), while others would slam the door
in her face, but she could not decide who would react in which manner, so she
said she had kept away from them all. Others had avoided shared friends in order
not to have to tell them about their marital separation.

Shared friends were mentioned only in the top half of the social class range.
Other couples had probably led separate social lives during their marriages.

Practical Help

Practical help by friends, neighbours or colleagues had been experienced by 47 per
cent of husbands and 48 per cent of wives. Unlike those who had had emotional
support, there was virtually no difference between the social classes, except that
classes I and II tended to be helped by 'friends' and classes IV and V by neighbours. Most neighbourly help was to those with children, and friends were again
significantly more likely to have helped the childless than those with children,
whether or not they had custody.

A common obstacle to rehabilitation for both husbands and wives was a reluctance
to start a new social life, and perhaps a fear of meeting new people. Once that
obstacle had been overcome with the aid of friends or relatives, a new life began
to look feasible. Some had had to be forced to go out in the evenings and to leave
the familiar domesticity in which they were insulating themselves from fresh human
contact and possible new hurt. It was not always easy for a single parent to go
out socially. 'People always say come and see us, but they don't pop up and see
you.' 'I don't like moping in other people's houses; they don't really know what
it's like,' indicated a desire for company at home rather than elsewhere.

Twelve respondents (two husbands and ten wives) had been grateful for friends,
neighbours or colleagues who had insisted on taking them out in evenings, even
when they had been reluctant to leave the security of their homes and face
strangers. 'It had been hard to take, and they helped me by going out with me and
lifting me out of myself.' Some were taken out for a drink, some to friends'
houses, some to dances. One wife said, 'If you're going to mope, you can do it
outside your home.' All had realised that this persistence by friends had led to a
turning point in their recovery from distress after separation. A wife of 22 had
refused to go out with the girls she worked with, until they came to her parents'
home to fetch her. 'They knew what was going on. After that, I was never in. I've
made so many friends since. Once I started on the road back, I couldn't seem to
stop.'

A woman whose marriage had lasted for six years had returned, with her small
daughter, to live with her mother, but had felt very lonely at first. Then a
couple up the road started taking her out with them on Saturday nights and she
felt better. She couldn't face the idea of going out alone to a pub, she said. Then
she began working in the hotel where her friends took her. 'The best thing I ever
did was getting the job helping in the bar,' because it got her out of the house
regularly; others had found a pub a useful place for making new friends, from
either side of the bar.

Another wife had expected separation to be easier, especially as she and her
husband had planned it. Her greatest difficulty had been 'going out on my own and
meeting people on my own. I don't actually go out very much; I'm a shy person ...
It is very difficult to make the effort.' She had been surprised to find that it
was far harder to go out alone after her marriage had ended than when she had been

unmarried. She had got used to being half of a couple and had not realised how
much she would miss having someone to do things with and to talk to and come home
to.

Others had had similar difficulties, and some had been able to offer reciprocal
support to friends whose spouses had left them. Only one expressed fear of the
opposite sex: 'Going out with boys was difficult; if they came near me, I shrank
away.'

Fourteen people (eight husbands and six wives) had accepted offers of accommodation from friends in flats shared with several others, some permanently and some
temporarily. The friends of two of these husbands had been workmates, in one case
offering a bed-sitter in a shared flat, and in the other a family home. One wife
had looked on a shared flat as a halfway stage from living with an aunt and uncle
to living alone. 'I felt I wanted to try and make my life on my own again.
Possibly if I'd gone straight from my family up here, I might have felt lonely.
Sharing, I got used to being alone gradually. It broke me in.' Another wife had
moved from her parents' home to share a flat with several girls because 'after
having been married, you get used to having a place on your own,' and she had not
felt at ease in her mother's house, although she had been away from it for only a
year and a half. Men had less to say about the friends who had offered them
accommodation, but had found them to be understanding and sympathetically inclined.

NEIGHBOURS

While many friends described in the study were also neighbours, some respondents
differentiated between the two and had specific comments to make about their
neighbours. More often than not, these were derogatory comments. 'Neighbour' was
more impersonal than 'my pal up the stair' or 'the lass next door'. It was not
easy, after moving house, to keep in touch with neighbours who had become friends.
'Before I left my husband, I was very friendly with the girl in the flat below.
But she has small children, and it's too difficult to visit. I was very sorry not
to continue seeing her.' Single parents with children often had to limit their
friendships to those with neighbours.

It was not surprising that 13 of the 18 respondents who had had practical help
from neighbours were parents with custody of their children. What was surprising,
though, was that a further 28 parents with custody of children had had no
practical help from neighbours. Only four (two men and two women) mentioned neighbours baby-sitting or keeping an eye on children. Others had had help by being
given food for the family, although this could be done in an almost apologetic
manner by a suggestion that the food offered was surplus to the requirements of
the donor. Other examples of practical help were housework or the loan of household equipment. One wife had given up the effort to mow the grass in her back
green and had gone shopping. On her return, she had found the grass cut and had
never found out who had done it.

Many claimed not to know any neighbours. In the more deprived areas, neighbours
were seen as not worth knowing, bearing out Klein's finding (1965) that help and
support in working class communities more often came from relatives than from
neighbours. 'We never associate with neighbours round here.' 'I have nothing to do
with the neighbours up here. I hate it here,' said a mother in a multi-storey top
flat, whose parents lived only across the road in a house which she saw as far
more desirable. A man who had lived in his local authority house for many years
and had a grown up family around him said, 'No one would want to mix with the
neighbours round here.' Many felt socially superior to their neighbours, but one
young wife had returned to her parents and siblings and a very dirty house and

described a neighbour as a snob.

The most common reply to a question about neighbours was, 'It's none of their business.' It was not only fear of stigmatisation nor even was it shying away from inquisitiveness about the marriage. Many had never known their neighbours during marriage. One man dismissed his neighbours by saying that he never saw them and that '95 per cent of the folk in this place are separated or divorced.' He attached stigma to others in his own situation. They could have helped each other by getting to know their neighbours, instead of staying in their ivory towers. Gorer found the divorced and separated to be more isolated from neighbours than others. In his sample, only 28 per cent of the divorced or separated knew most of their neighbours by sight, compared with 46 per cent of the single and 38 per cent of the married (Gorer, 1955).

Two neighbours had given professional help, one being a solicitor and the other a nurse whose advice on treating depression had complemented that of the family doctor. Only six husbands and eight wives described emotional support from neighbours but some friends who had given such support were also neighbours.

Neighbours, in particular, did not know how to react to the remaining spouse when one had left home. 'They used to talk to me quite freely, but now they don't.' 'There's a couple along the landing I don't see very often. It takes her all her time just to say hello. I get the impression she's avoiding me. I think she's just embarrassed.' 'Some people cut me now and others are embarrassed.' One woman's neighbours did not ask her outright where her husband was, but transparently side-stepped the issue by asking whether his car was away being repaired.

Many neighbours were curious or inquisitive, especially when a married son or daughter returned alone to their parental home. Then, it could be the parents who felt embarrassed when they were called on to make explanations.

> Neighbours were a difficulty in fact. Going back to my
> mother's house, she felt it more when they said "I see R's
> back staying with you". I don't think she ever gave a
> conclusive answer yet. Very few people were brusque enough
> to say "have they split up?"

> They were not cruel. It was just avid curiosity. My mother
> wouldn't satisfy the neighbours' curiosity directly. She
> got a couple of very good friends to spread the news, and
> sympathy started pouring in.

Another young wife had gradually realised that her parents' neighbours must know why she was living at home again:

> I was embarrassed from the point of view I was sort of
> hiding from people I hadn't seen for a time. I would cross
> the road instead of stopping to speak to them.

One wife had felt embarrassed by the presence of neighbours who had been very understanding during the difficult end of her marriage, but she now wanted to escape from them. 'They used to see him coming in late, and they knew what he did to me. They couldn't understand how I'd put up with him for so long.'

There was also some initial embarrassment shown by old acquaintances when they were first told of a broken marriage. This was especially so if they had un-wittingly been tactless by asking apparently innocuous questions about the other spouse, not knowing that he had left home. 'People say "how are you getting on

with your house?" or "how is your husband?" It's like stabbing you in the back
with a knife.'

Eleven respondents reported experience of neighbours who had made censorious
remarks. A secretary who had seen 'a change in some people which was hurtful'
quoted, as illustration, a friend who had said, 'It really is sad the way you're
running around with men.' A young mother had a neighbour who openly disapproved of
her leaving her husband: 'Once she tried to make out I wasn't there, but she knew
I was standing there and said something that really hurt.' Similarly, a young
father was offended by his mother's neighbour who told him he was 'a bad devil'
for leaving his wife and son. 'She was nosey. I've never come face to face with
her since I gave her a piece of my mind.'

The most unkind example of neighbours' behaviour was given by the father of two
young children. His girlfriend, who had not been involved in the breakdown of his
marriage, had come to live with him and the children soon after they had moved
house. At first, neighbours had assumed she was his wife. When they discovered
that she was not, they openly shunned her. 'Some will cross the road to avoid her.
Some are embarrassed and some have made a judgment.' Two families had stopped
their children from playing with his, to the bewilderment of all the children. One
wife had suffered taunts because she had been mentally ill.

> Some of the neighbours don't like me because of having
> nervous breakdowns. Some of the neighbours are terrible, but
> I'm no moving because of them ... I used to sit and cry, but
> I've got over that ... They think you're locked up in padded
> cells, but I was never locked up. They're lucky it doesn't
> happen to them ... You should see people with their tongues.
> They just gossip. Usually it's the people that talk about
> other people that shouldn't talk.

She found it embarrassing when neighbours asked why she hadn't got custody of her
children, although her illness probably made that impossible. A wife who had taken
in a neighbour's husband for a whole year was most indignant that:

> Everybody I'd been sort of friendly with just turned their
> backs on me. I was friendly with the girl nextdoor - it was
> her husband I went with ... I never split up her marriage ...
> The lassie up the top flat and another lassie down the road
> both turned their back on me and said my husband was such a
> quiet fellow and how could I do that to him.

She not only lost her husband and her neighbours, but she also lost her new
partner who returned to his own wife.

Neighbours who were wise after the event or who passed on unwanted information
were also hurtful. A middle-aged husband had been told by a neighbour that his
wife had been going out with other men for many years. A young wife had been
informed by her nextdoor neighbour that her husband was going to divorce her. 'I
had plenty problems ... but if my husband was going to divorce me, he'd have told
me first.' And another wife said, 'There were two couples we sort of knew, one up
the stair and one down, but it turned out they weren't very nice. One of the other
neighbours up there used to phone me up and tell me half my clothes were in their
houses and she'd tell me who got what.'

Neighbours seemed to have been more hurtful than colleagues or other acquaintances.

COLLEAGUES AND EMPLOYERS

Solace of a socially acceptable kind was found by those who were able to immerse
themselves in their work. It was described by a nurse ('if I had been purely a
housewife, I would have gone under, but with a ward of forty beds, I could cut off
from the situation'), a woman social worker ('my job has been the greatest support.
Looking back, it was having to get up in the morning and get on with the job that
was the most help') and a service engineer ('I got on with my job. I've enjoyed my
job more in the past two years').

Work had had a salutary effect on some, but there were others who were aware that
the quality of their work had suffered and that colleagues had quietly covered up
for them. This probably was not apparent to them until afterwards, when they
realised that allowances must have been made by understanding employers or
colleagues. A professional man said, 'In retrospect, I suspect I was not really
very efficient at my work, sitting taking pills.' A wife who had found it helpful
to have to get up in the mornings was sure that her work had not been allowed to
suffer, but that her colleagues had almost certainly covered up for her, especially
when she was 'crying my eyes out in the toilet ... Really I must have got a hell
of a lot of support from my colleagues but it was done in a very subtle way. I'm
still getting it probably.' A manual worker knew that worry had made him short-
tempered: 'I seem to snap at people at work. I lose the head.'

The employed in the sample were 54 husbands (90 per cent of all the husbands) and
45 wives (75 per cent). Some of the employed wives had only part-time jobs but all
of these husbands and wives had had colleagues to whom they might have turned for
help. 37 per cent of the employed husbands and 53 per cent of the employed wives
had had some kind of help or support in this way. 24 per cent of the husbands and
42 per cent of the wives in employment had had emotional support at their work; 24
per cent of the husbands and 33 per cent of the wives had had practical help.

Some employers had allowed time off work for visits to lawyers. Others had given
practical advice over 'what not to do with my personal life', finding a lawyer,
househunting or even accompanying an employee to look at houses available. One
(with his wife's approval) had given a home for a week, while others had given
meals with an opportunity to talk, had reduced workloads or altered working hours
on request. Two employers were said to have been sympathetic because they had had
marriage problems of their own.

Fewer had turned to colleagues or workmates than to employers. It had not generally been difficult to explain that a marriage had broken down. One wife had
grasped the nettle firmly and had told all those with whom she worked closely:
'I've got something to tell you. I've left my husband.' That way, she ensured that
no one would ask questions and she'd heard that there had been no gossip.

Explanation of Changed Status to Friends and Others

Many had been conscious of living in a no man's land after separation. They
considered that they were not married or single, nor yet divorced and yet they
felt the need to explain their status to new friends or acquaintances or, indeed,
to convey their changed status to people they had previously known. It seemed to
be difficult to start any new friendship on an honest footing without making people
shy away from them. Several had been on the defensive, anticipating a sense of
stigma.

It was often a problem to know just how to make clear a partnerless status. An
unemployed labourer, aged 37 and living alone, had noticed local women in the

street and had found himself wondering whether they were unattached. He knew that
there were a great many single parent families in the area, but he did not know
how to start a conversation, let alone a friendship, with any of the women he saw.
'You can't stop someone in the street and ask if they're single.' If he had been
less conscious of his own status, he would probably (especially as he was a
compulsive talker) have had no qualms about chatting to strangers. A woman of 34
found that the first question a man would ask her at dances was whether she were
married or single. She was conscious of being neither, and therefore of missing
opportunities to make friends with men. Matters were later simplified for her when
she could say that she was divorced.

Some solved the problem by claiming to be single, even before divorce, especially
if they were looking for new partners. 'It was awkward at the beginning of the
separation. Thinking specifically about girlfriends, I didn't want to say "how do
you do, I'm separated, can I buy you a drink?" I acted as though I was single.'
And: 'When I meet other people ... I give the impression I'm just not married. It
hits me most when I have people back. They say "who are the children? (in a
photograph) ... oh, I didn't know you were married".' Complications arose if a new
friendship were leading to marriage, and the earlier marriage had not been
mentioned. 'It was difficult to approach her at first and explain.'

Two opposite reactions were reported by one wife and one husband. 'Their attitude
is so surprising, because they're not surprised. I'm always surprised that people
expect it. Any embarrassment is within myself. But I still have a thing about it.
It's not something I'm proud of. Not something I want to boast about. I try, when
I meet anyone not to hide it.' And the man: 'I still find when people start a
conversation with me they bite off their tongue when they realise they're talking
to me about divorce. But it doesn't bother me.'

Some described unwelcome or unfriendly reactions to their marital breakdown, not
only from the opposite sex. They knew that they were seen to be unattached and
available as potential partners, while still struggling to detach themselves from
previous partners. Already in an ambiguous position, they resented behaviour which
made their readjustment even more difficult. One wife sensed a mixture of envy and
disapproval. 'I'm very aware this is a couple-based society. Certain married women
can be a bit hostile, especially at dinner parties. They feel threatened. It
happens with women who aren't happy themselves.' And another said 'they take you
out one night and expect you to hop into bed the next night. Men think if you've
been married, you can't do without it which is rubbish.' A man had had difficulty
in accepting the attitude of married friends: 'It's funny, married men take a
different view. They don't like you as a friend. Possibly they look on you as a
rival.' A middle-aged wife had found that her friends' husbands were 'a wee bit
more free - there's just a wee bit feeling that you're a bit loose.' Similar
difficulties were highlighted by Chester's sample (Chester and Streather, 1972).

Miscellaneous

Two people had had valuable and sympathetic assistance from an unexpected source.
One, a husband, had been 'in a dreadful state, a real financial mess' and had
explained to his bank manager that he was having difficulties because of his
broken marriage. He was relieved to find the bank manager 'very non-judgmental -
he was terrific'. The other, a wife, had opened a bank account at an unknown bank
two months before leaving her husband. After separation, she had explained to her
new bank manager that her husband had promised her £1000 from the eventual sale of
their house. She was astonished to be offered a bank loan of this sum 'on my
husband's say-so'.

Two husbands had consulted booklets about divorce, which had clarified some points for them. One of them, with custody of his children, had also read textbooks about child care.

Finally, one man, unemployed and with custody of his children, claimed to have no friends except for his fifteen tropical fish, which provided him with 'a hobby'.

Conclusions

'Everyone has a chum they can talk to,' was the opinion of a hotel chambermaid. Many had shared her experience, but 29 per cent had had no practical help or emotional support from friends, neighbours or colleagues. Some had not necessarily lacked friends, but had not leaned on them. 'That's not what friends are for,' said one wife. Whether or not they had colleagues or could describe anyone as a friend, they all lived in a well populated area and must have had many neighbours. Contact with neighbours other than friends had been minimal. Embarrassment or a possible sense of stigma had affected some relationships, removing potential sources of help at a crucial time. There seemed to be room for more good-neighbourliness and self-help groups.

CHAPTER 9

CONCLUSIONS AND RECOMMENDATIONS

It is probable that not all sources of help were explored in any single interview and that respondents failed to recall some instances of help. My recorded impression of what was relevant may not always have coincided with what the respondents thought important (cf. Anderson, 1972).

The general impression from the majority of interviews was that there had been less bitterness, less unhappiness and less traumatic shock than is popularly thought to exist after marriage breakdown. For many, any suffering had been during the marriage and it was before, rather than after, separation that they might have sought help. Future research could usefully investigate such behaviour prior to marital separation. For instance, Dobash and Dobash (1980) described some fruitless requests for help made to family and professionals by wives who were desperately trying to escape from their husbands' violence.

There had been less need than I had expected for supporting services outside the family. Most respondents had lived near enough to their families of origin to find there a source of emotional support which was not only easily accessible but was available at all times. This was a more personal service than any agency could provide, however professional.

In an examination of the choice between expert bureaucratic help and family support, Litwak (1965) argued that the extended family has many advantages over the experts: the family is more readily and continuously available, intermediaries are not required, and family members may share the same personal values and already be on terms of familiarity with each other, so that there are no worries about confidentiality. Litwak pointed out that family support, unlike professional help, may be given even when it has not been requested, because the members of a family are in a position to know what is happening and what is required.

Evidence of the availability of an extended kin network, to provide mutual aid and social activities, was shown by Sussman (1965) to be in a number of American studies into family relationships and support systems. Reciprocity, which is a recurring theme in other studies, is possible between members of an informal network, whether of family or of friends, but is not normally possible between a person in need and a professional helper.

When informal networks prove unsatisfactory, if they are judged to be unsuitable for confidential disclosures or if they are not used for any other reason, then professional help is more likely to be sought (Mayer and Timms, 1970). Perceptions of available services may also be influenced by the client's or his family's experiences of other services, even though there may be no direct similarity between the types of service (Rees, 1978). The present study did not compare, for each individual, the total of informal help experienced with the total of expert help experienced. Such a comparison would have shown whether doctors, social workers and marriage counsellors (and particularly the last) were approached when informal networks had failed.

If the sample had not been limited to divorces where both partners lived in the same city at divorce, extended families might have been less accessible and other contacts might have had increased importance. So it was not possible to investigate fully Anderson's suggestion that 'it is of particular interest to study what happens to those who have no relatives to perform any particular function' (Anderson, 1972). A larger sample would have been required, in order to discover the principal sources of help used by those who had no mothers, fathers or siblings or who, having some of these relatives, did not turn to them for help. Such individuals were in a minority in this study and the sub-group would have been too small for any conclusions to be drawn.

For the majority, support from fathers or siblings depended on whether they had support from their mothers: it was unusual to reject mothers in favour of others in the family. It is a useful pointer, therefore, to examine those who had had no emotional support from their mothers. There were 68 such respondents, of whom 26 husbands and 19 wives had had mothers available, and 13 husbands and 10 wives had had no mothers during the period of separation. Most had found alternative informal emotional support from one or more sources outside the family (23 from friends, 17 from colleagues and 9 from neighbours), but a few had found it elsewhere within the family (for instance, 8 from fathers, 6 from sisters and 3 from mothers-in-law). Also, 17 of them had found their doctors helpful, but mostly in addition to friends, neighbours or colleagues. Seven who had had no support from mothers claimed to have had no informal emotional support from anyone.

While friends and colleagues were the principal alternatives to mothers, it was interesting that those who were not supported by mothers had had fewer sources of informal emotional support than those who were (a mean of two sources compared with a mean of 3.3). This suggests that those who found their mothers supportive tended to turn to others also. Possibly they based their expectations of other potential helpers on their experiences of their mothers, but this was not investigated. Expectations of social work may be based, as Sainsbury (1975) pointed out, on previous experiences (good or bad) of informal family support.

A factor which seemed to reduce any search for help was the apparent feeling of fatalism. If a spouse had left home, whether or not after joint agreement, the remaining spouse often gave the impression that there had then been only two viable alternatives. Either they had tried to persuade the deserting spouse to return, or they had accepted that the marriage had finished. There did not seem to have been many attempts to understand the reasons for what had happened, or to examine their own behaviour. Events were seen in black and white. There was seldom any account of a search for interpretation. Emotional support had been required mainly to combat loneliness, which was often pinpointed as a major problem.

Several respondents suggested that only those who had themselves experienced a broken marriage were qualified to offer sympathy and support. A divorced friend was expected to be more helpful than a doctor or a marriage counsellor. Mayer and Timms (1970) also found a belief that anyone who had not suffered similar difficulties would be unable to understand a client's problems, and Parkes (1972) wrote that 'people who have themselves experienced a major bereavement may be particularly well qualified to help the bereaved'. The belief that those who have suffered similarly can give the best support has led to the formation of many self-help groups, for instance for alcoholics, gamblers, depressives, single parents, parents who have lost a child or people with specific disabilities. These groups appear to be very successful but do not appeal to all who are eligible to join them.

Respondents divorcing in the late 1970s might have needed less emotional support than an earlier generation would have done. The possibility, for the first time, of divorce by consent may have helped some couples to part more amicably than if they had been forced to found their divorce on a matrimonial offence. Probably, too, more support would have been needed in the past when divorce was more difficult to obtain. On the other hand, there may also then have been more silent suffering because of the stigma attached to a broken marriage.

For many marriages which break up, there are probably sufficient readily available sources of help from an informal network of family and friends. For others, there is a continuing need for support from doctors, social workers and marriage counsellors. Few respondents saw any of these as potential sources of emotional support. Few had sought help from any individual or agency over problems of children caught up in divorce. More information is needed about the perceptions and experiences of such children.

Doctors were expected to be concerned with physical ills, social workers with children or the elderly and marriage counsellors with mending marriages.

SOLICITORS

Solicitors come into a different category from other sources of help, since they are a necessary part of the divorce procedure. Their duty is to their clients as individuals and not to the marriage partnership.

There was evidence of a simple trust and a lack of understanding on the part of respondents, and the vast majority expressed satisfaction with their solicitors' services. Nevertheless, there is plenty of scope for the legal profession to explain more clearly what is involved in divorce. It is not enough to give information, however painstakingly; it is necessary to check for comprehension. Solicitors can become so familiar with divorce procedure and language that they can forget how little some clients are likely to understand. Training in the behavioural sciences and in interviewing techniques should be given to solicitors and to their unqualified staff who meet the public. A day conference, with visual aids to illustrate clients' difficulties, could clear away many misunderstandings.

Divorce work may be tedious and repetitive but it is more skilled than is sometimes admitted. Since a fixed fee is often charged (and especially for Legal Aid work), there is seldom time available to spend with clients apart from the direct business of discussing divorce. No doubt some solicitors would disagree and say that they do discuss the possibility of reconciliation, but that is seldom seriously considered by a client who has reached a solicitor. Conciliation is a different matter and can be far more time-consuming. The Finer Committee (1974, para 4.288) defined reconciliation as 'assisting the reuniting of the parties' and conciliation as 'assisting the parties to deal with the consequences of the established breakdown of their marriage'.

The role of the solicitor, here, is to ensure that clients thoroughly understand the consequences of divorce. In particular, the implications of financial awards (or the lack of them) for children and for spouses were often found to have been misunderstood in this study. Too many respondents, both husbands and wives, failed to appreciate the long-term effect on their income of making or receiving financial provision. Wives tended to be philosophical about any shortage of money. For some, later on, aliment from husbands might cease or be spasmodic and would certainly be worth less. Some financial hardship might be avoided if solicitors explained more fully the importance of financial agreements, especially where they affect children. Awards to wives will indirectly affect their children.

Access to or by the absent parent is arranged by parents or by lawyers, usually without taking into account the children's wishes. Whatever arrangements are made by the adults, contact with the absent parent is likely to diminish with time. In one quarter of the families in the present study, one parent had lost touch with the children by the time of divorce. Some parents had been surprised to find no mention of access in their divorce certificates: they had assumed that it would be automatically granted. Divorcing parents should have it very carefully explained to them, in writing, that there will be no provision in their divorce for access by the absent parent unless this is specifically requested. It may well be that there is often no need for such provision: either the parents trust each other to give and to allow access according to their private arrangements, or one parent may not wish to see the children. Whether the children wish access is another matter. Little is known about children's views on access, nor how long or how often access arrangements, made before divorce, continue after divorce.

A recently formed divorce court welfare team in Bristol found that by the time of divorce, in one third of the families referred to them (who, in turn, constituted approximately one third of all divorces in the Bristol registry) the circumstances of the children were different from those described in the divorce petition (Fraser, 1980). This must mean that elsewhere (where there is no such welfare team) many divorces are being granted with out-of-date information about the children. The recommendation of the Royal Commission on Legal Services in Scotland (1980) to refer divorces with children to children's panel reporters, would provide an ideal opportunity to assess the position of children of divorcing parents.

Next, there is the problem of legal communication. Legal documents are in complicated language; a short and simple translation should be supplied. The preamble to a summons is in archaic language and should be greatly simplified, as was done in England for High Court writs in June 1980. Letters from solicitors can be difficult for clients to understand, and information given by a solicitor at an interview may not be understood by the client.

It should be made very clear to husbands, in advance, that they are likely to be liable for the considerable expenses of divorce actions even when their wives, as pursuers, have been financially assisted by Legal Aid. A suggestion by the Royal Commission that no expenses be awarded against divorce defenders would satisfactorily deal with this problem, if implemented.

There was evidence that social classes IV and V are reluctant to consult solicitors and, if they do so, to be significantly less satisfied than others. Two lessons can be learned from this: that there should be more branch offices of legal firms in working class areas and that extra care should be taken in ensuring that consultations and communications have been understood.

Defended divorces are still heard in open court, as are any others where a judge requires a hearing. For those who have to attend court, there should be simple instructions, preferably in a printed and illustrated leaflet so that they may better understand the layout of the court and the nature of the proceedings. They should not be allowed to be the only participants with no prior knowledge, as chief actors on a stage without a rehearsal. The present procedure results in

witnesses being too preoccupied with the setting to be able to concentrate on what
is being said.

Possibly the Law Society of Scotland was claiming too much for some solicitors'
skills in issuing a leaflet Marriage Problems? which concludes:

> Above all a solicitor will be more than just your lawyer;
> he will also be your counsellor, financial adviser and some-
> one to whom you can turn in that all too difficult period
> when a marriage is breaking up.

DOCTORS

When support is not available from family or friends, and approach has to be made
to a profession or an agency, then doctors are likely to be the first choice
because it is socially acceptable to consult a doctor.

In theory, everyone has a doctor and can judge whether he is a helpful person to
talk to. Some respondents considered that their doctors would be too busy to
listen, too old to understand, or not interested in marriage difficulties. These
respondents sought help elsewhere and did not want medication. But half of the
sample did turn to their doctors, usually with complaints of 'nerves' or sleeplessness. They expected, and received, prescriptions for tranquillisers, as
Chester (1973), Ferri and Robinson (1976) and Parkes (1972) had also found. Many
did not consider it part of the doctor's role to investigate the underlying causes
of their symptoms and some thought it inappropriate to embark on elaborate explanations. At times, the doctor's acceptance of a problem at its face value was in
itself reassuring.

Nevertheless, a doctor who found time to listen was appreciated, and more support
might have been given in this way to patients who had chosen their doctors as
sources of help. It is true that the fault lay partly with the patient who claimed
to be suffering from 'nerves' but preferred not to reveal the cause. Most of those
who had been conscious of emotional as well as professional support from their
doctors had usually not talked to their mothers.

Nearly half of the husbands and a quarter of the wives who had consulted their
doctors considered them to have been unhelpful. Husbands were not only significantly
less likely than wives to have consulted their doctors after marital separation,
but, having done so, were less likely to have found them helpful. Dissatisfaction
with a doctor's services often sprang from disappointment that the doctor appeared
not to be willing to listen. Possibly male patients were more inhibited about
making known their need to talk, and doctors did not expect men to require that
kind of support.

Doctors seemed, from the evidence presented, not always to have realised that
marriage breakdown was the cause of 'nerves' or mental stress; alternatively, they
may have been more percipient than the patient realised, but have chosen not to
risk time-consuming consultations by asking too many questions. Tranquillisers may
be all that a patient requires, but an opportunity to talk to the doctor or one of
his colleagues could sometimes be therapeutic. A positive offer of continuing
support, either from the doctor himself or in the form of an immediate introduction
to another worker in the same building might be found to be more valuable than a
repeat prescription for tranquillisers. This course of action would be easier in a
large health centre, with paramedical workers available, than in a small general
practice. In the latter case, a doctor could perhaps ask a patient to return at a

time when he had a social worker or marriage counsellor available on a sessional basis.

Many general practitioners have insufficient training in dealing with psycho-somatic problems and, additionally, some lack the aptitude or inclination to do so. Doctors learn to treat most patients 'by the methods of illness-centred medicine and only a few with the new techniques of patient-centred medicine' (Balint, 1973). The result, according to Clyne (1973) can be that 'most if not all doctors feel the need for and are trying to use patient-centred medicine, but by tradition and clinical training are fettered to illness-centred medicine'.

CLERGY

There was little evidence that ministers or priests had carried out their trad-itional pastoral role, partly because very few respondents belonged to any church. Even the minority who have a church connection are sometimes reluctant to speak to their own clergy about marital breakdown. They may feel shamed by the sense of failure, and not want to speak to someone whose respect they value. Clergy, there-fore, do not always hear of marital difficulties within their own congregations. An expanding role for churches could be to use their halls to provide informal meeting places where people could make new friends over a cup of coffee. Several respondents voiced the need for a community centre, perhaps with a 'motherly figure' present.

SOCIAL WORKERS

Social workers were believed to be too busy to have time to spend on marriage or personal problems and, as Mattinson and Sinclair (1979) found, it was rare for anyone to approach a local authority social work department for help with a specific marital problem. Mattinson and Sinclair reported that many long-term high-priority clients did have marital as well as other problems but that social workers saw themselves as offering practical help, often in terms of crisis relief. They did not find it easy to make time to deal with emotional problems, and they tended to avoid doing marital work with multi-problem families. The authors suggested that, if they are to help with marital problems, social workers should either concentrate on 'the clients they cannot avoid and whom other agencies are often unwilling to accept', or take on smaller case-loads with close super-vision.

In the present study, those few who had sought social work assistance had mostly made purely practical requests, such as help in rehousing or in placing children in day nurseries. It had not occurred to them to talk about marital breakdown, or its effects on their children. Others, who had been assigned social workers because of difficulties with children after marriage breakdown, had dissociated themselves from such problems, seeing these as belonging to their children and being the responsibility of the social worker to solve. Social workers were suffered and were criticised for not giving practical help, for being too young and inexperienced or for a lack of continuity of care because of mobility within the profession. However, their intervention had been appreciated by more than half of those who had had experience of social work services, whether or not requested.

Although social workers were not expected to discuss emotional problems, there is still an important role for them in cases of marital breakdown. Training in child care makes them ideally suited to offer support to children of a broken marriage, where those children might feel bewildered or rejected. If social workers could discuss with parents before divorce the possible consequences for children (as happens in the Bristol court welfare service), and offer a preventive service, then children might run into fewer difficulties as a result of parental separation. There was evidence in this study that parents had avoided explanations to their children and had also denied that their children had suffered in any way as the result of parental separation. Some parents were more concerned with their own status than with observation of their children. They had hoped that skirting round the subject would obviate the necessity for explanations. The recommendations of the Royal Commission on Legal Services in Scotland (1980) could, if implemented, go a long way towards solving this difficulty. The Royal Commission envisaged at least one interview with one or both parents and, in certain cases, with the children themselves. This duty could well be the responsibility of social workers.

MARRIAGE COUNSELLORS

Marriage counsellors, like social workers, are usually unknown as individuals and their very anonymity may deter people from approaching them. It takes considerable courage to make, and then to take up, an appointment with a stranger in order to expose one's personal life. It is widely, but falsely, assumed that marriage counsellors are marriage menders. The ten per cent of this sample who had been their clients may not have been typical clients, since all had become divorced, and most had seen a counsellor after deciding to end the marriage. If any of the 90 per cent who had not sought counselling had done so, possibly some would have formed a better understanding of what was happening to their marriage relationships, whether or not they had proceeded to divorce.

There were basically two kinds of marriage guidance client in this study: those who made a single visit in the hope of either bringing their spouse to heel or of obtaining sanction for their actions, and those who expected to talk about and to explore their problems. Those in the first category may not have needed counselling but, since they had chosen to consult that agency, the agency was fulfilling a need, even though no magic wand was waved. 'I knew that if I went to a marriage counsellor, at least I would have made the effort.' The second category included those for whom the special skills of marriage counselling were appropriate, and some of them had achieved a better understanding of their relationships. It was noticeable that any who could, with hindsight, put their expectations into words had looked for someone who would listen or would give 'advice' or offer 'a solution'. Husbands, who had been less appreciative than wives of their doctors' services, were far more likely than wives to have found marriage counsellors helpful. Men, perhaps, were less inhibited about talking to a counsellor than to their doctor.

Some had broken off counselling when it became painful to them, even when their own professional work should have led them to expect such an experience. It had been helpful to talk to a sympathetic stranger instead of to family or friends, but difficult to respond to sensitive probing. The exploration of feelings can be an uncomfortable process and its value difficult to appreciate. The most usual reason for either breaking off counselling or for not seeking it in the first place was that the other spouse had refused to see a counsellor. 'She turned it down flat and I didn't think there was any good out of going on my own.' While a crumbling marriage relationship clearly involves at least two people, one partner in a marriage can gain valuable emotional support from a marriage counsellor, even in preparation for divorce or after divorce. Few people realise either that one partner alone can be helped or that counsellors do not try to preserve all marriages. Several respondents had rejected the idea of seeking support from a marriage counsellor because they did not want to save their marriage and saw that as the underlying purpose of marriage counselling. For instance, 'I think they might have helped. Before we broke up, I did mention it, but it was too late.' 'I ruled it out as an impossibility. We had both made an effort and we were incompatible.'

There are misconceptions about marriage counselling but these must be partly perpetuated by a lack of effort to correct them. It should not be impossible to devise means of letting potential clients understand something of the nature of counselling. It is important, too, to make known the location of counselling premises, the opening hours, whether it is necessary to make an appointment, whether there is a waiting list, whether both spouses must attend together, how long a counselling interview might last and whether a fee is payable. Local marriage guidance councils could benefit from each other's experience in identifying obstacles in the path of potential clients who may have difficulties in making appointments to see counsellors (Marquis, 1975; Mitchell, 1976). The problem was brought to the attention of the Scottish Marriage Guidance Council by their vice-chairman (Duncan, 1974) when she wrote 'it is undeniable that we are not grasping effectively the reaching of those in trouble ... Until we sit down and think this through, we are failing.'

Some counsellors, having undergone selection and training, suffer a shortage of work and therefore lack an opportunity to gain experience. In Scotland, in 1978, 138 marriage counsellors gave an average of 49 counselling interviews each, compared with a recommended annual commitment of 120. Most marriage guidance councils in Scotland have always been cautious about publicity.This has been for a number of reasons, including the strange one that publicity might bring in too many of the very clients whom counsellors have been trained to help. It is time that they sold their wares in the market place. They must eradicate the mystique which surrounds them. If the service is valuable, it should be made better known, in an effort to halt the steady annual decline in the numbers of clients in Scotland, including Edinburgh, where the present research was undertaken. There was a decrease of 22 per cent from 1975 to 1978 in the annual number of clients in Scotland, and a 24 per cent decrease in the annual number of Edinburgh clients from 1973/4 to 1978/9, compared with a 5 per cent increase in National Marriage Guidance Council clients, 1974 to 1978.

Marriage guidance councils would also benefit from research into three areas:

(1) expectations and impressions of counselling by their clients;
(2) perceptions held by potential clients – this study has shown that some people had misconceptions which prevented them from seeking counselling; and
(3) the reasons why many first and – a different problem – subsequent appointments are not kept.

In 1975, James reported that a project to reduce the number of broken first appointments in Glasgow had been planned but rejected by a committee. She noted a reduction in broken first appointments when the client had to take some initiative in confirming an offer of an appointment, as happens in some small councils in Scotland.

Marriage counselling skills have developed over the years, but approaches by marriage guidance councils to the problem of an escalating divorce rate have not. Hooper (1976) suggested a swing in emphasis to 'active, accessible and positive counselling in which the problems which are produced by the clients are delineated sharply and attempts made to help the couple solve them'. He also recommended the development of crisis-intervention counselling on the Australian family court model, or a 'therapeutic approach with the emphasis on client-oriented action and initiation' and he cast doubt on the value (for some clients) of the pattern of 'the periodic spacious interview'. He followed up his call for more flexibility by pointing out that 'personal service ... is a growth industry' in which there are now other kinds of counsellor and he criticised the air of 'withdrawn sanctity' within marriage guidance (Hooper, 1978).

The traditional weekly, hour-long interview was established to meet the needs of people with marital difficulties thirty years ago. Nowadays, marriages are four or five times more likely to end in divorce and the partners often do not have time for a long and careful examination of marriage problems. Many marriage partners, judging by the experience in this research, suddenly find themselves with a broken marriage. They have needed either instant practical help or a sympathetic listener, or both. Marriage counsellors should consider offering an easily available walk-in service with a quick, diagnostic, first interview (described as intake counselling in some English marriage guidance councils). A client who gains immediate satisfaction from such a service is more likely to recommend it to his friends than one who undergoes a long, traumatic series of counselling sessions. And personal recommendation is the best advertisement for a service.

Marriage counsellors have long emphasised their non-directive approach, but Parry-Jones (1978) suggested a combination of 'insight counselling with more directive methods' and greater use of authority. He questioned whether the present selection and training procedures (only slightly different in England and in Scotland) can equip counsellors to undertake sufficient responsibility for bringing about change in their clients. He recommended a diagnostic approach and 'a behavioural form of marital therapy and counselling ... (with) less emphasis on interpretation and intellectual understanding'.

The recent consultative document by the Working Party on Marriage Guidance (1979), in recognising the initiative and courage required by clients who consult marriage counsellors, recommended greater flexibility in counselling for 'the less articulate or socially less confident client' and stressed the need for the service to be more available and more comprehensive. Better co-operation with other agencies was also recommended.

The balance of outcome for marriages in difficulties has changed since marriage counselling was first offered. Not only do an increasing number end in divorce, but the frightening rapidity with which a marriage can nowadays move from conflict to divorce demands a response to Professor Hooper's and Dr Parry-Jones's ideas. Marriage guidance councils pioneered a specialist service but, as long ago as 1968, Dominian wrote that in marriage counselling, 'social, material and health problems should receive adequate and effective attention' before inter-personal relationships are examined. The Wolfenden committee pointed out that an established voluntary organisation which is 'exclusively identified with one particular need or type of service runs the risk of resting on its laurels' (Wolfenden, 1978).

Some new approaches to marital conciliation (as opposed to reconciliation) have been made recently. New organisations too have developed, for instance, the Bristol Courts Family Conciliation Service (not to be confused with the new Bristol divorce court welfare team) and the Divorce Counselling and Advisory Service in London. The first provides a conciliation service for clients referred by solicitors, enabling agreement about the future of children or about financial provision to be reached without expensive litigation; the second is a crisis-intervention service for those whose lives are disrupted by the dissolution of their marriage.

SUMMARY

Throughout the accounts of help from the professions or from voluntary organisations, there runs the theme of practical advice being more acceptable from
these sources than emotional support. Expectation of help is often linked to the
presentation of practical difficulties. Therefore, marital problems are more often
taken to the Citizens Advice Bureaux than to marriage guidance councils (Wallis,
1974). The desirability of co-existing practical help and emotional support runs
through other studies (e.g. Bayley, 1973; Mattinson and Sinclair, 1979; Sainsbury,
1975). All who see themselves as offering emotional support or counselling should,
perhaps, look at the possibilities of gaining the confidence of clients or patients
by first dealing with practical difficulties. The crisis which prompts a request
for help may blind the client to the value of skilled ongoing support. Until a
client's most pressing practical needs are met, he may feel some uncertainty about
the role of an agency. For the same reason, his first contact with the agency,
whether with gate-keeper or case-worker, is of importance in giving him confidence
(Hall, 1974; Mansfield and Smith, 1974; Reith, 1975).

The Wolfenden committee on the future of voluntary organisations (1978) defined
the role of statutory or voluntary social services in relation to the care provided
by informal networks as the provision of replacement, relief or reinforcement. The
committee considered that, in planning future services, statutory and voluntary
organisations should take more account of the available informal systems of care.
They should make more effort to support the community in its helping role, instead
of concentrating on direct services to those in need (Bayley, 1973). Organised,
but informal, community care can complement both professional care and support
from family and friends (Humphries, 1976) and could profitably be developed on a
basis of reciprocity of services between client and helper (Abrams, 1978).

All that many respondents had described in this study was a need to talk to a
sympathetic listener who would not ask awkward questions, but would offer re-
assurance. Many had found this support through an informal network of family,
friends and colleagues. More could have been helped to an understanding of what
divorce would mean to them and to their children, if they had been more
knowledgeable about social work and marriage counselling services.

APPENDIX   INTERVIEW CHECK LIST

Children	Spouse	Doctor
Health	Children	Health Visitor
Housing	Mother	Social/welfare worker
Employment	Father	Minister
Money	Mother-in-law	Employer/colleagues
	Father-in-law	Lawyer
	Sisters	
	Brothers	DHSS
	Other relatives	

CUSTODY

ACCESS	New partner	Marriage guidance
	Friends	Citizens' Advice Bureau
	Neighbours	Samaritans
		Other

REFERENCES

Abrams, P. (1978). Community care: some research problems and priorities. In *Social Care Research* (papers and report of a seminar sponsored by the DHSS). Bedford Square Press, London.

Adams, B.N. (1968). *Kinship in an Urban Setting*. Markham, Chicago.

Anderson, M. (1972). The study of family structure. In E.A. Wrigley (Ed.), *Nineteenth Century Society*. University Press, Cambridge.

Balint, M. (1973). Research in psychotherapy. In E. Balint and J.S. Norell, *Six Minutes for the Patient*. Tavistock, London.

Bayley, M. (1973). The mentally handicapped and their professional helpers. *Brit.Jnl. of Social Work*, 3, 349-363.

Becker, H.S. and B. Geer (1960). Participant observation: the analysis of qualitative field data. In R.N. Adams and J.J. Preiss (Eds.), *Human Organisation Research*. Dorsey Press, Illinois.

Benney, M. and E.C. Hughes (1956). Of sociology and the interview. *American Jnl. of Sociology*, 62, 137-142.

Blaxter, M. (1976). *The Meaning of Disability*. Heinemann, London.

Bott, E. (1957). *Family and Social Network*. Tavistock, London.

Brandwein, R., C. Brown and E.M. Fox (1974). Women and children last: the social situation of divorced mothers and their families. *Jnl. of Marriage and the Family*, 36, 498-514.

Byrne, P.S. and B. Long (1976). *Doctors talking to patients*. HMSO, London.

Cartwright, A. and W. Tucker (1967). An attempt to reduce the number of calls on an interview inquiry. *Public Opinion Quarterly*, 31, 299-302.

Cartwright, A. and W. Tucker (1969). An experiment with an advance letter on an interview inquiry. *Brit.Jnl. of Preventive and Social Medicine*, 23, 241-243.

Chester, R. (1973). Health and marital breakdown: some implications for doctors. *Jnl. of Psychosomatic Research*, 17, 317-321.

Chester, R. (1975). *The Adjustment of Women to Divorce*. Final report to SSRC. (HR 703).

Chester, R. and J. Streather (1972). The stigma of divorce. *Social Service News*, 2, 12-15.

Church of Scotland (1969). *Divorce Law Reform*. Report of the social and moral welfare board to the General Assembly of the Church of Scotland. Church of Scotland, Edinburgh.

Civil Judicial Statistics, Scotland (CJS) for 1975, 1976, 1977, 1978. Cmnd.6577, 6926, 7365, 7762. HMSO, Edinburgh.

Clive, E.M. and J.G. Wilson (1974). *The Law of Husband and Wife*. Green, Edinburgh.

Clyne, M.B. (1973). The diagnosis. In E. Balint and J.S. Norell (Eds.), *Six Minutes for the Patient*. Tavistock, London.

Cohen, S. and L. Taylor (1977). Talking about prison blues. In C. Bell and H. Newby (Eds.), *Doing Sociological Research*. Allen and Unwin, London.

Court of Session Statutory Instruments 1978 No. 106 (S.5) *Act of Sederunt*. Rules of Court Amendment No.1 (Consistorial Causes).

Dean of Faculty of Advocates and President of Law Society of Scotland (1978). *Affidavit Evidence in Undefended Divorce Actions*.

Denning Committee (1947). *Final Report of the Committee on Procedure in Matrimonial Causes*. Cmd.7024. HMSO, London.

Divorce (Scotland) Act (1938). HMSO, London.

Divorce (Scotland) Act (1976). HMSO, London.

Dobash, R.E. and R.P. Dobash (1980). *Violence Against Wives*. Open Books, London.

Dominian, J. (1968). *Marital Breakdown*. Penguin Books, Harmondsworth.

Douglas, J.W.B., J.M. Ross and H.R. Simpson (1968). *All our Future*. Peter Davies, London.

Duncan, D. (1974). The obstacle race. News and Views, 24, 1. Scottish Marriage
    Guidance Council, Edinburgh.
Dunnell, K. (1979). Family Formation. HMSO, London.

Eekelaar, J. and E.M. Clive (1977). Custody after Divorce. SSRC, Oxford.
Elston, E., J. Fuller and M. Murch (1975). Judicial hearings of undefended divorce
    petitions. Modern Law Review, 38, 609-640.

Ferri, E. and H. Robinson (1976). Coping Alone. NFER, Windsor.
Finer Committee (1974). Report of the Committee on One-Parent Families. Cmnd.5629.
    HMSO, London.
Fraser, D. (1980). Divorce Avon style - the work of a specialist welfare team.
    Social Work Today, 11, xxx, 12-15.

Gavron, H. (1966). The Captive Wife. Routledge and Kegan Paul, London.
George, V. and P. Wilding (1972). Motherless Families. Routledge and Kegan Paul,
    London.
Gibson, C. (1974). The association between divorce and social class in England and
    Wales. Brit.Jnl. of Sociology, 25, 79-93.
Goldstein, J., A. Freud and A.J. Solnit (1973). Beyond the Best Interests of the
    Child. Free Press, New York.
Goode, W.J. (1956). After Divorce. (Reprinted as Women in Divorce, 1965). Free
    Press, New York.
Gorer, G. (1955). Exploring English Character. Crescent Hall, London.

Hall, A.S. (1974). The Point of Entry. Allen and Unwin, London.
Harris Committee (1948). Report of Departmental Committee on Grants for the
    Development of Marriage Guidance. Cmd.7566. HMSO, London.
Hart, N. (1976). When Marriage Ends. Tavistock, London.
Hooper, D. (1976). Yesterday's counsellors for tomorrow's problems? Marriage
    Guidance, 16, 147-153.
Hooper, D. (1978). Counselling: the meaning, the message and the market-place.
    Marriage Guidance, 1978, 18, 4-8.
Hopkinson, A. (1976). Single Mothers - the First Year. Scottish Council for Single
    Parents, Edinburgh.
Humphries, B. (1976). Only Connect. Guild of Service, Edinburgh.

James, J. (1975). First appointment failures. News and Views, 27, 11-12. Scottish
    Marriage Guidance Council, Edinburgh.
Jarvis, F. (1974). Probation Officers' Manual, 2nd edition. Butterworth, Woburn.
Journal of Law Society of Scotland (1979). Notes: Affidavit evidence in undefended
    divorces. 24,3.

Keith, R. and G. Clark (1977). The Layman's Guide to Scots Law, Vol.2, Divorce.
    Gordon Bennett, Edinburgh.
Kilbrandon Committee (1969). Report of the Committee on the Marriage Law of
    Scotland. Cmnd.4011. HMSO, Edinburgh.
Klein, J. (1965). Samples from English Culture. Routledge and Kegan Paul, London.

Lasch, C. (1979). Haven in a Heartless World. Basic Books, New York.
Litwak, E. (1965). Extended kin relations in an industrial democratic society. In
    E. Shanas and G. Streib (Eds.), Social Structure and the Family. Prentice-Hall,
    Englewood Cliffs.
Lopata, H.Z. (1978). Contributions of extended families to the support systems of
    metropolitan area widows. Jnl. of Marriage and the Family, 40, 355-375.
Lord Chancellor's Office (1977). Undefended Divorce.

Mace, D. (1948). Marriage Counselling. Churchill, London.

McGregor, O.R., L. Blom-Cooper and C. Gibson (1970). <u>Separated Spouses</u>. Duckworth, London.

Mansfield, P. and J. Smith (1974). What a reception! <u>Social Work Today</u>, <u>5</u>, 354-356.

Marquis, B. (1975). Appointments secretary: innovations. <u>News and Views</u>, <u>27</u>, 12-13. Scottish Marriage Guidance Council, Edinburgh.

Marris, P. (1958). <u>Widows and their Families</u>. Routledge and Kegan Paul, London.

Marsden, D. (1969). <u>Mothers Alone</u>. Allen Lane, London.

<u>Matrimonial Proceedings (Children) Act</u> (1958). HMSO, London.

Mattinson, J. and I. Sinclair (1979). <u>Mate and Stalemate</u>. Blackwell, Oxford.

Mayer, J.N. and N. Timms (1970). <u>The Client Speaks</u>. Routledge and Kegan Paul, London.

Merton, R.K., M. Fiske and P. Kendall (1956). <u>The Focused Interview</u>. Free Press, Illinois.

Merton, R.K. and P. Kendall (1956). The focused interview. <u>American Jnl. of Sociology</u>, <u>51</u>, 541-557.

Mitchell, A. (1976). Puzzle - find a counsellor. <u>News and Views</u>, <u>28</u>, 10-11. Scottish Marriage Guidance Council, Edinburgh.

Mitchell, A.K. (1980). <u>An Exploratory Investigation into Sources of Help Used Before Divorce</u>. M.Phil thesis, University of Edinburgh.

Morris, P. (1965). <u>Prisoners and their families</u>. Allen and Unwin, London.

Morris, P., J. Cooper and A. Byles (1973). Public attitudes to problem definition and problem solving. <u>Brit.Jnl. of Social Work</u>, <u>3</u>, 301-320.

Moyes, B.A. (1976). <u>Perceptions of Pregnancy</u>. Ph.D thesis, University of Edinburgh.

Murch, M. (1975). <u>Evidence to Home Office Marriage Guidance Working Party</u>. Unpubl.

Murch, M. (1977 and 1978). The role of solicitors in divorce proceedings. <u>Modern Law Review</u>, <u>40</u>, 625-638 and <u>41</u>, 25-37.

Murchison, N. (1974). Illustrations of the difficulties of some children in one-parent families. In <u>Finer Committee Report</u>, Appendix 12. Cmnd.5629-1. HMSO, London.

Office of Population Censuses and Surveys (OPCS) (1970). <u>Classification of Occupations</u>. HMSO, London.

Parkes, C.M. (1972). <u>Bereavement</u>. Tavistock, London.

Parry-Jones, W.Ll. (1978). Change to survive? Reflections on the future of marriage counselling services. <u>Marriage Guidance</u>, <u>18</u>, 75-83.

Quarantelli, E.L. (1960). A note on the protective function of the family in disasters. <u>Marriage and Family Living</u>, <u>22</u>, 263-264.

Rees, S. (1978). <u>Social Work Face to Face</u>. Edward Arnold, London.

Registrar General Scotland (RGS). <u>Annual Reports</u> for 1977 and 1978. HMSO, Edinburgh.

Reid, R. (1979). Divorce in the Sheriff Court. <u>Jnl. of Law Society of Scotland</u>, <u>24</u>, 447-452.

Reith, D. (1975). I wonder if you can help me? <u>Social Work Today</u>, <u>6</u>, 66-69.

Rowntree, G. and N.H. Carrier (1958). The resort to divorce in England and Wales, 1858-1957. <u>Population Studies</u>, <u>11</u>, 188-233.

<u>Royal Commission on Law of Divorce</u>. First report (1853). Command Paper 1604. HMSO, London.

<u>Royal Commission on Legal Services in Scotland</u> (1980). Cmnd.7846. HMSO, London.

<u>Royal Commission on Marriage and Divorce</u> (Gorell Commission) (1912). Cd.6478-6479. HMSO, London.

<u>Royal Commission on Marriage and Divorce</u> (Morton Commission) (1956). Cmd.9678. HMSO, London.

Sainsbury, E. (1975). <u>Social Work with Families</u>. Routledge and Kegan Paul, London.

Scottish Law Commission (1967). _Divorce: The Grounds Considered._ Cmnd.3256. HMSO,
    Edinburgh.
Social Work (Scotland) Act (1968). HMSO, London.
Sussman, M.B. (1965). Relationships of adult children with their parents in the
    United States. In E. Shanas and G. Streib (Eds.), _Social Structure and the_
    Family. Prentice-Hall, Englewood Cliffs.
Swinton, K. and L. Clark (1978). Divorce - new style. _SCOLAG, 23,_ 170-171.
    Scottish Legal Action Group, Dundee.

Thornes, B. and J. Collard (1979). _Who Divorces?_ Routledge and Kegan Paul, London.
Townsend, P. (1957). _The Family Life of Old People._ Routledge and Kegan Paul,
    London.
Townsend, P. and D. Wedderburn (1965). _The Aged in the Welfare State._ Bell, London.

Wallis, J.H. (1974). Matrimonial problems and the Citizens Advice Bureaux.
    Marriage Guidance, 14, 334-337.
Wolfenden Committee (1978). _The Future of Voluntary Organisations._ Croom Helm,
    London.
Working Party on Marriage Guidance (1979). _Marriage Matters:_ a Home Office
    consultative document. HMSO, London.

Young, M. and P. Wilmott (1957). _Family and Kinship in East London._ Routledge and
    Kegan Paul, London.

INDEX

Abrams, P., 116
access to children, 5,36,41,88,92-3,96, 110
   see also children
accommodation, see housing
Act of sederunt, 10
Adams, B.N., 78
advice, see help
advocates
   at court, 10,40-1
   drafting summons, 8
   welfare reports, 5,96
age at divorce, 21-2,32,67,69,72,88
age at marriage, 21,63
alcohol, 43-4
Alcoholics Anonymous, 43,60
Anderson, M., 107,108
approach to respondents, 12-13,17,25-8

Balint, M., 112
bank managers, 105
Bayley, M., 116
Becker, H.S. & B. Geer, 18
Benney, M. & E.C. Hughes, 18
bereavement, 2,61,95,108
Blaxter, M., 1-2,43
books about divorce, 106
Bott, E., 2,17,72
Brandwein, R., C. Brown & E.M. Fox, 1
Bristol Courts Family Conciliation Service, 115
Bristol divorce court welfare team, 110
brothers, 78-82
   compared with parents, 78,82
   helping bereaved, 61
   percentage of sample helped by,30,31
Byrne, P.S. & B. Long, 48

Cartwright, A. & W. Tucker, 13 (bis)
Catholics, 48,63,89
Chester, R., 3-4,11,12,22,42,45,111
Chester, R. & J. Streather, 105
childlessness, 24-5,32,37,88,97-8
children, 90-6
   explanations to, 94-5,113
   finance, 37-8,52,85,109-110
   housing, 68,95
   in divorce, 24-5,96,109,110
   none, 24-5,32,37,88,97-8
   percentage of sample helped by,30,31
   problems, 50-1,112
   welfare, 5,10,95-6
   see also access, custody
children's hearings, 51,95,110
church, see clergy

Church of Scotland, 7,48-9
Citizens Advice Bureau, 59-60,116
   percentage of sample helped by,30
Citizens Rights Office, 60
Civil Judicial Statistics, 7,8,21,22,23
clergy, 5,48-9,63,112
   percentage of sample helped by,30,31
Clive, E.M. & J.G. Wilson, 6,7,8,15
   see also Eekelaar, J. & E.M. Clive
club for divorced and separated, 60
Clyne, M.B., 112
co-habitation, see new partners
Cohen, S. & L. Taylor, 18
colleagues, 97-106
   compared with mothers, 108
   first mentioned source of help, 32
   percentage of sample helped by,30,31
committee on
   grants for development of marriage guidance, 55
   one-parent families, 1,109
   procedure in matrimonial causes, 55
   voluntary organisations, 2,61,115,116
community care, 60,112,116
computer analysis, 29
conciliation, 109,115
   service, Bristol courts family, 115
councillors, district, 54
counsel, see advocates
counselling, 4,115
   see also marriage counsellors
Court of Session
   divorces heard at, 6,9
   observation at, 9
   pursuers' experiences, 39-41,95-6
   Rolls of Court calling lists, 11,14
custody of children, vii,5,25,32,36,68, 91,95-6,101
   see also children

daughters, 61
   see also children
Dean of Faculty of Advocates, 10
defenders, vii,20-8,36-7
   interviewed, 11,15,26-7
   reactions to divorce, 14
delay, legal 35
Denning committee on procedure in matrimonial causes, 55
Department of Health and Social Security, 52-3,
   aliment claimed by, 37
   percentage of sample helped by,30
divorce
   age at, 21-2,32,67,69,72,88
   defended, 9,10,15,110